# Quaker Voices
## on
# Mental Health

Q

First Published in Great Britain in 2025 by Quacks Books

7 Grape Lane, Petergate, York YO1 7HU
Tel: +44 (0)1904 635967
Email: design@quacks.info
Website: radiusonline.info

Quacks Books is an imprint of Radius Publishing Ltd

A CIP catalogue record for this book is available from the British
Library.

ISBN Paperback: 978-1-917562-05-8
EBook ISBN: 978-1-917562-08-9

Set to the size of 176 x 250mm
printed by offset on a one hundred gsm chosen for its sustainability.

Cover design based on a painting by Craig Barnett

# ACKNOWLEDGMENTS

This book would not have been possible without the committed support and contributions of many people throughout the months of development, from the initial idea to the book in your hand.

First and foremost we thank wholeheartedly the chapter authors listed in CONTRIBUTORS on pp.vi - viii.

As well, we are extremely grateful to the Sessions Book Trust and the Quaker Mental Health Fund for their generous funding.

Our warm thanks also go to Martin Nelson and Rebecca Houghton of Quacks the Printers in York, who have been unfailingly helpful throughout; to Judy Roles for her skilled and dedicated support; to Martin Dickinson for proof reading; and to the editor Rosemary Roberts, backed up by 'critical reader' editors Rob Griffiths and Chrissie Williams.

And to you the reader. We hope you find this book thought-provoking and a resource for discussion and action about the issues raised by our contributors. If you feel able to recommend the book to others and spread the word about Quaker Voices on Mental Health, please do!

# Contents

# CONTRIBUTORS

Quaker Voices on Mental Health is a Quaker Recognised Body, a growing membership network that warmly welcomes new Friends and Attenders. Members can safely explore issues in mental health, guided by Quaker testimonies to equality and truth and informed by the legacy of William Tuke (founder of The Retreat, York). We create opportunities for Friends to meet together in person or virtually in a spirit of worship: to uphold one another in our different capacities, and for discernment on matters associated with mental health. We explore the relationships between spirituality, creativity and mental health wellbeing, promote awareness and understanding of mental health issues across Britain Yearly Meeting, and hope to inform pastoral care at Local, Area and Yearly Meeting levels. We contribute a Quaker Voice on aspects of mental health and wellbeing policies and practices in Britain today.

**Lucy Aphramor** is a radical dietitian and poet currently in post as Workplace EDI co-ordinator with the Quakers . They developed the health-gain approach, Well Now, linking self-care and social justice, informed by their practice with marginalised communities and personal experience. They are a member of the Food Ethics council and have won NHS, charity, and professional awards for their work.
http:www.lucyaphramor.com

**Moya Barnett** is twenty three years old and has been a Quaker since she was a young child. She is currently volunteering with refused asylum seekers in London and building community with marginalised people.

**Jo Baynham** is writing from his own personal experience as a youthworker, not in his professional role as a Quaker Youth Development Worker. His specialisms are in contemplative spirituality and compliance in adventurous settings. Jo is particularly interested in fresh expressions of Quakerism and growing the confident voice of Quaker communities. Jo attends Rawdon meeting.

**Angela Greenwood** is a Leigh-on-Sea Quaker, an Experiment with Light practitioner, and a retired Educational Psychotherapist. She still occasionally finds herself prompted to take initiatives towards a more thoughtful and inclusive education system for our most vulnerable children - including through Quaker Voices on Mental Health.
https://www.angelagreenwood.net/

**Max Kirk** (they/them) writes mostly from their personal experience, but they are also a researcher and youth worker, and that feeds into their thoughts and reflections here. They grew up in Yorkshire and now live a semi-nomadic life, working and living and loving in the UK and beyond while they complete their doctorate.

**Eddy Knasel** joined Bristol Area Quaker Meeting in the mid-1990s. He led a weekly dementia aware café on behalf of Horfield Quakers which ran with financial support from the Quaker Mental Health Fund successfully for three years prior to the COVID pandemic. Eddy has been involved in Quaker Voices on Mental Health since its inception.

**Mark Lilley** of Lincoln Local Quaker Meeting says "Personal stories like mine about mental ill-health make a crucial contribution to developing Quaker approaches and responses based on our core principles and Testimonies".

**John Miles** of Nailsworth Quaker Meeting (Gloucestershire) has almost 50 years' experience of living with various close relatives who experienced mental illness. Being a Quaker has helped him sustain his role as a carer. John was trustee Director of The Retreat (York) Psychiatric Hospital from 2013 to 2019.

**Alison Mitchell** is part of Exeter Quakers. She worked for many years as a social worker within the mental health system, then for the Quaker Mental Health Fund. She now sits on the Mental Health Tribunal.

**Sheila Preston** was an Occupational Therapist in mental healthcare for many years. She worked in Dementia care, and feels passionate about supporting individuals and their carers to live their fullest lives possible. As a Quaker, this fits with her values and guides her in her pastoral care role at Aylsham Meeting in Norfolk.

**Rosemary Roberts** worships at New Earswick Meeting in York. She holds a postgraduate diploma from the Tavistock Clinic UK in Psychoanalytic Observational Studies, and a PhD for which she researched wellbeing development from birth to three in the home. Now retired, her work has been mainly with the youngest children and their families. Her chapter is informed by them; and by her current concern for children's mental health.

**Zillah Scott** has been a Quaker for over twenty years and worships at Sheffield Central Meeting. She is studying for a diploma in Social and Therapeutic Horticulture with Thrive.

**Beverley Smith** says "My name is Bev and I've been a Quaker for over 20 years. I have lived on and off with depression for most of my adult life".

**Mike Wash** of New Earswick Meeting, York says "This chapter looks historically at the legacy of the Tuke family on mental health today; from an informed Quaker perspective of present-day services". Previously he was Trustee Director at The Retreat York & Clerk to The Retreat Benevolent Fund (now the Quaker Mental Health Fund).

### The Quaker voices in Chapter 11 'Mental health behind bars'

This is a collective contribution by three Quaker Prison Chaplains and four residents who each attend Quaker Meetings in different prison settings. Two of the residents became Quaker and have been accepted into Membership since coming into prison. This has been an important commitment for them, even though they have years ahead of them in custody. They are all serving life or a lengthy sentence ranging from a minimum term of 9 to 25 years.

For each of them, being accepted by and belonging to a faith community within prison has been an important part of their mental well-being on their journey of self-examination, change and rehabilitation. The Quaker Prison Chaplains who support them are part of a multi-faith chaplaincy team in each prison which offers faith and pastoral care to all faiths and none on a daily basis. As well as the faith that grounds their ministry, the Quaker Prison Chaplains bring significant life experience from careers in teaching and counselling; but the most valued gift they offer is deep listening and a compassionate presence.

# INTRODUCTION

This book, 'Quaker Voices on Mental Health', is a call to bring before Friends the urgent need for a renewed focus on mental health within the work of Britain Yearly Meeting. It forms a part of the work of the Quaker recognised body, Quaker Voices on Mental Health.

The book is a series of twelve chapters by different Friends, on different Quaker perspectives of mental health. It has been written for fellow Friends, not predominantly for the general public. The aim is to raise awareness within the Society about current mental health issues and their relevance to us as Quakers today. With the intention to stimulate conversations among Friends about mental health, we hope Friends of all ages in Quaker meetings will benefit; and perhaps many of those with whom readers come into contact in their Quaker lives of worship and witness.

Throughout the book, the term 'carer' refers to the many and varied voluntary roles in the chapters, not to professional carers. Also, in the chapters about youth-work and about food, the contributors write not about their professional roles working for BYM, but from their own personal perspectives.

Readers may notice that throughout the book some basic themes come up again and again, often around Quaker testimonies to peace, truth, community, equality and social justice; even though they may be referred to differently depending on what the chapter is about. Common ground across the chapters is also evident in awareness of the need for 'kinder ground'; and nearly all chapters include ideas and suggestions to support local meetings. Above all, these chapters are a call to action.

Quaker Voices on Mental Health's Steering Group would like to emphasise that all these common elements have happened purely fortuitously, not having been planned or foreseen by us. Towards the end of 2024 we put out the idea of a book to highlight the urgent need for a renewed focus on mental health among Friends, to be ready for BYM in May 2025. Offers to contribute were invited, and Friends who expressed an interest in time - sometimes having been suggested by other F/friends - were simply asked to write about mental health in relation to their chosen subject, from their Quaker perspective. In so many ways the response has been astonishing, bringing us to a strong sense that everyone involved was upheld in this work.

For further information about the activities of Quaker Voices on Mental Health, including the newsletter, forthcoming activities and ways to get involved, please go to **www.quakervoicesonmh.org.uk**. Thank you.

Quaker Voices
on
Mental Health

The Steering Group for
Quaker Voices on Mental Health:

Lizzie Davies, Rob Griffiths, John Miles, Nicholas Paton Philip, Sheila Preston,
Rosemary Roberts

March 2025

# Chapter 1

## The Tuke family's contribution to mental health and its relevance today

### Mike Wash

*Mike's perspectives in this chapter about the Tuke family are both historical and reflective. The chapter describes how, starting in the eighteenth century, generations of the Tuke family from William onwards responded to the need for better mental health with ground breaking and innovative Quaker initiatives. These were followed by further developments for mental health in the nineteenth and twentieth centuries. The chapter continues with more Retreat history in the twenty-first century, ending with a moving reflection on the question: "As Quakers, are we doing enough?"*

## Hannah Mills' story

The little known story of a Quaker woman called Hannah Mills tells us how she was a catalyst to the development of an humane approach to mental illness.[1] Hannah lived in Leeds with her husband Samuel who was a "stuff maker" (a weaver of a type of woollen cloth). They lived in the Hunslet area which was described at the time as impoverished but rich in artisan textiles. Likely to be living on a low income with a growing family, life would have been difficult.

Hannah's husband, Samuel, died in 1786. Six months later Hannah gave birth to a son, making her a widow with 5 children at the age of 38. In the next 2 years, 3 of her children died and one of her remaining children was disabled. Hannah, through grief and poverty, despite being supported by Friends, was eventually admitted to the York Asylum with 'melancholy' on the 15th March 1790. During her time in the York Asylum Friends attempted to visit on several occasions but were denied access due to her being "of an unfit state of mind to receive strangers". She died on the 30th April that same year. Her manner of death is unknown; records were lost in a fire of suspicious circumstances in early 1800's.[2] Subsequent inspections of the Asylum found 13 women sharing a small room that was soiled with their own excrement with

---

1    https://www.herstoryyork.org.uk/wp-content/uploads/2024/03/Hannah-Mills.pdf
2    The abuses at the York Asylum later became the centre of a great controversy. A national investigation in 1813-14 led to questions in Parliament. Some of the asylum records were burned in a suspiciously timed fire and two different sets of financial accounts were discovered. The resulting scandal led to substantial reforms in the way the hospital was run. http://www.historyofyork.org.uk/themes/georgian-architecture/bootham-park-hospital-formerly-york-lunatic-asylum

a complete lack of natural light and cases found whereby the women were harassed and abused by male inmates and staff keepers.[3]

It is likely that Hannah experienced these types of conditions and they were a factor in her demise. These circumstances became known to William Tuke, and were the motivating factor that started him down the road to mental health reform. He was instrumental in waking the consciences of Quakers as to the immorality of treatment of the mentally ill of those times.[4]

# The Tuke family and the Retreat

In 1752 William Tuke (1732-1822) had taken over the family firm of wholesale tea and coffee merchants, which had been founded by his Aunt Mary Tuke in 1725. He, his son Henry (1755-1814) and his grandson Samuel (1784-1857), developed this successful company, as well as devoting their time to many religious and philanthropic activities. The company was eventually bought by Henry Isaac Rowntree in 1862, which was the start of the global chocolate manufacturing giant.[5]

In the Spring of 1792 William Tuke, Lindley Murray, and other members of the Society of Friends, proposed the establishment of a 'retired habitation' near York for treatment of persons afflicted in mind. The 'retired habitation' was built through the donations of members of the Society of Friends throughout the country, and was opened on May 11th 1796, when it received the name of "The Retreat." The original structure still remains as the central portion of the Retreat buildings. Although now not a hospital, the therapeutically designed grounds, Quaker burial ground and the Retreat as a mental health outreach therapeutic centre remain.

Henry, William's son, and Samuel his grandson, both played an active part in managing the Retreat. Samuel's son James Hack Tuke (1819-1896) in his turn aided in the management of the York Retreat and later focused on famine relief aid to Ireland. James's brother Daniel Hack Tuke (1827-1895) co-wrote the important treatise *A Manual of Psychological Medicine*'in 1858 and became a leading physician dedicated to the study of insanity. The Tuke family were instrumental in the formation and development of what became known as 'Moral Treatment' in a homely environment, treating persons of ill mind with respect and kindness. This became a pioneering model for many institutions worldwide.

---

3        Kathleen Jones, *Lunacy, Law and Conscience 1744-1854: The Social History of the Care of the Insane* (London: Routledge & Kegan Paul, 1955), https://theretreatclinics.org.uk/
4        https://fabricatingfiction.wordpress.com/2018/09/21/why-we-should-all-have-the-same-dream-as-william-tuke-bekind/
5        https://www.rowntreesociety.org.uk/explore-rowntree-history/researching-rowntree/

In 1813 Samuel Tuke, the grandson of the founder, wrote the *Description of the Retreat* in which he set forth the principles of the treatment there adopted. This valuable book was destined to have a far-reaching influence.[6] It was most favourably received by reviewers, amongst whom Sydney Smith in the *Edinburgh Review* drew attention to the success attending the humane methods of treatment, foreshadowing what was to come: "an example has been set of courage, patience and kindness, which cannot be too highly commended, or too widely diffused, and which will gradually bring into repute a milder and better method of treating the insane."

There is one case described in the book that epitomises the regime of care. This was the case of a man in his forties of 'herculean proportions' presented at the front entrance of the Retreat in sackcloth and chains having had a history of violent mania. He was received into what was then a homely environment, chains removed, bathed and invited to sit with other patients and attendants for supper. He was given his own room and was told of the clear parameters of what was and was not acceptable.

Apart from an occasional outburst of verbal threat from which he was calmly talked down, he became increasingly positive and active in the home life of The Retreat and was discharged four months later. There was no restraint and no medication only kindness, respect and a recognition that by relating to this man as a whole person and appealing to his positive sense of self then he could be helped back to living a healthy life back in society.[7]

The Retreat has, therefore, the distinction of being the first institution in England where the insane were treated in accordance with modern humane methods. It was not until fifty years after its foundation that reform in treatment was assured throughout the kingdom by the passing of the Lunacy Act of 1845, and the appointment of the permanent Lunacy Commission.

The Tuke family's determination to highlight the plight of the mentally infirm and to establish a form of care that became a world wide model of excellence is one of William Tuke's greatest achievements. This essential perspective of approaching the whole person remains at the forefront of care and is supported by the many effective medical treatments through pharmacology and talking therapies.

---

6     *Description of The Retreat an Institution near York of The Society of Friends*, Process Press, 1813

7     Ibid

# Twentieth century developments

Despite Quakers advocating treating the person humanely and respectfully, perhaps it was inevitable that the medical model of diagnoses and treatment with medication, electro convulsive therapy, neurosurgery (frontal lobe lobotomy) and restraint has been seen as the solution to large unwieldy wards often struggling with too few staff even to achieve the basics of care. This toxic mix of closed institutions, poorly resourced and often dominated by minimally researched evidence based treatments, led to the inevitable enquiries when either whistle blowers, relatives or undercover reporting highlighted examples of abuse. In 1967 the Whittingham Hospital was investigated after student nurses reported many cases of abuse and poor care. The investigation led to recommendations for change, although it seems likely that the abuse continued in many hospitals. This report was a case study highlighted in my student nurse days.

Between 1971 and 1989 my career as a psychiatric nurse culminated in becoming a nurse tutor. During this time I was also witness to many 'uncaring' practices within the large institutions in which most of our student nurses were working at the time (prior to Care in the Community which closed en masse many of the large psychiatric hospitals in favour of smaller care homes in the community). My colleague and I were motivated to write an updated text to guide future nurses in the spirit of recognising the importance of a patient centred approach.[8] The book, *Psychiatric Nursing Skills* became the best selling text book in psychiatric nursing and is still used today. This is testament to the first principles Samuel Tuke elucidates as central to care: each person being unique and treated as a whole person, with respect, empathy, and kindness. Despite the advocacy of patient centred care, abuse of these principles was still too often reported.

In Sept 2022 The Edenfield Centre in Manchester was reported by an undercover BBC Panorama team for physical abuse, inappropriate restraint and seclusion, swearing at and ridiculing patients in a toxic culture. The Taplow Manor Hospital, Maidenhead was investigated for systematic abuse and poor care in March 2023. The Lampard enquiry is still ongoing. This concerns the death in unusual circumstances of 1500 children, young people and adults within the North and South Essex Mental Health Trust. It includes reports of physical, mental and sexual abuse of residents in 2021. And most recently the death of 3 people at the hands of Valdo Calocane in June 2023 has highlighted the many failings of the Nottingham Mental Health services. The enquiry indicated that many warnings went unheeded as regards Calocane's

---

8  Dexter, G. and Wash, M. *Psychiatric Nursing Skills - A Patient Centred Approach* 2nd ed. 1995. Thomas Nelson

mental state.[9]

I ask myself, how does this happen in today's society of vigorous inspection and emphasis on high care standards? There is certainly a lack of adequate resources and appropriate living/caring environments; but surely also a lack of 'Quaker' practice.

# Twenty-first century developments

The Retreat still remains, not as a hospital but as outpatient centres both in York and Manchester. Quaker principles continue to be interwoven into its philosophy of care, based on values of compassion, collaboration and community building, and overseen by a predominantly Quaker Board.[10]

There is also The Quaker Mental Health Fund[11], originally established by Quakers in 1919 as The Retreat Benevolent Fund. Its formation was at a time when The Retreat was struggling financially to the extent that they were having to send back to 'Asylums' patients that were once subsidised by an endowment fund. Shortly after the first world war, due to the cost of living, increases in nurses pay, essential repairs and maintenance to The Retreat, there were over 60 patients who were costing more than the income provided. A national appeal for funds was agreed by Meeting for Sufferings, and further funds were added by donations, bequests and annual subscriptions. This fund was then used to subsidise Quakers who needed treatment at the Retreat, but were unable to pay for it. However, very little of the money raised was spent, because the charitable objectives had been too narrowly defined, relating only to treatment at The Retreat. In 2019 the objectives were widened to include grants for Quakers who find difficulty accessing the right mental health care, and for Quaker-led projects designed to result in better mental health outcomes generally. Meanwhile a long-standing group of Friends committed to working for better mental health care had formed, and Quaker Voices on Mental Health was formalized.

Part of the vision at this time was to enable a supportive network involving the many disparate Quaker groups showing concern for the care of the mentally ill. A post was created in order to pull together these groups, to raise the profile of the importance of effective care, and to highlight the potential for support and improvement through initiatives already sponsored by the

9       Whittingham and others: https://eprints.bbk.ac.uk/id/eprint/41918/9/41918a.pdf; Edenfield Centre: https://www.england.nhs.uk/north-west/our-work/publications/ind-investigation-reports/independent-review-gmmh-nhs-ft/; Taplow Manor: https://news.sky.com/story/taplow-manor-mental-health-unit-that-treated-young-people-worse-than-animals-shut-down-after-sky-news-investigation-12924477; Lampard Enquiry: https://lampardinquiry.org.uk/; Valdo Calocane: https://www.bmj.com/content/386/bmj.q1796

10      https://theretreatclinics.org.uk/

11      Quaker Mental Health Fund https://www.quakermhfund.uk/

Quaker Mental Health Fund. One of these initiatives was to form a group who would come together in a yearly conference, in person and online: to explore best practice, share learning and experience, and once again highlight the principles of respect and acceptance seen by Quakers as relevant today as they were in the pioneering days of William and Samuel Tuke. Today, Quaker Voices on Mental Health holds these annual gatherings, and publishes regular newsletters on matters related to mental health concerns and creative developments. It brings together a national network of Friends who have concerns about mental health and who feel led to serve and give witness to this cause.

## As Quakers, are we doing enough?

It seems that a Quaker view of the essentials for treating mental illness has not changed a great deal over 225 years. Here is my own view of what this is: *Treat any person in distress with respect and kindness. Listen not just to words but to the whole person. Welcome them into a homely environment and give them space to be themselves without restraint or fear. Include them equally with others; and build on their strengths so they can grow with confidence to live a peaceful life in society once more.*

To what extent is this a reality in the mental health care facilities and services available today? There have been significant improvements in available therapies and patient/client-centred care. However, there are still too many individuals - lost souls - hiding alone behind walls, too many parents shocked and devastated by their children committing suicide, and too many tormented minds imprisoned in our justice system because of the inadequate provision of more appropriate alternatives to that system.

Out of mental distress can come despair but it can also create insights and a multitude of different perceptions of how the world is seen, if we take time to listen. Unique interpretations of life can be rich in the deep understanding of self. Our own spirituality and how we relate to the world is often created in paintings, storytelling and poetry.[12] Those in mental distress may experience the world as a fearful place or perhaps see it in a uniquely complex way that clashes with expected norms of society. It is for this reason that we advocate a way of creating environments where those who need them feel safe, feel listened to, and are helped to work through their journey to a place where they can once again be accepted and supported to be who they really are.

The stillness and reflective space in a Quaker meeting is precious; these can be moments of meditative thought, a process of connecting to important values that are part of our personal identity. This internal dialogue with

---

12      Simon Miles https://theidentityparade.org/about-the-identity-parade/

oneself (or 'God') can create insights that nurture the soul; they can generate a positive sense of well being that nourishes our mental health. Being Quaker is also for me being part of a community that strives to be non judgemental and contributes to welcoming anyone to explore their spiritual journey in an environment of equality and empathy. Mental ill health can be experienced in a cloud of lonely personal anguish and grief - a sense of loss or losing oneself, contributing to despair and loneliness. A counter balance to this can be experienced by being part of a Quaker community where you never have to feel alone and always have the option of being with those who will genuinely be there for you. This spirit, over two hundred years ago, led to Quakers showing the world how mental health care based on acceptance, dignity and respect, may heal the most disturbed of us.

For me, being Quaker is a recipe for positive mental health. Religion is all too often seen through jaundiced eyes as divisive and the source of conflict between belief systems and cultures. Yet the world religions have more in common than differences. The Religious Society of Friends has at its core a central belief that there is that of God in everyone. Whatever a person's understanding or belief is, the central message is that everyone has the potential to be the best a human can be in terms of giving and receiving love and compassion. The capacity to demonstrate these caring traits for ourselves and for each other are fundamental to our mental health.

## Can we identify with the Tuke family?

Today poor mental health care, evidenced by inadequate facilities and lack of resources, is all too evident. And as in the time of the Tukes, today we can work to support the development of homely environments, where each individual is cared for with respect and dignity. We can show what best practice in the treatment of mental illness looks like, in so many ways. But are we doing enough?

Do Quakers today share William Tuke's concern about mental health?

# Chapter 2

## Honouring Dark and Light

### Beverley Smith and Mark Lilley

*This chapter is based on the personal testimonies of Bev and Mark given to the Quaker Voices on Mental Health Forum in Manchester in the autumn of 2024. They speak about living with their own mental illness in ways that encompass both dark and light, which was the theme of the event.*

## Bev's experiences of Dark and Light, and what has helped her

*Growing up in a fundamentalist Christian church*

I was brought up in a fundamentalist Christian church with very rigid thinking and teaching about darkness and light. One of the first hymns that I learned to play on the piano was 'Yield not to temptation', and the first verse goes like this:

> *Yield not to temptation, for yielding is sin;*
> *Each vict'ry will help you some other to win;*
> *Fight manfully onward, dark passions subdue;*
> *Look ever to Jesus, He will carry you through.*

So darkness was something to overcome and subdue, and within the teaching of my church it was associated with the concept of sin and the devil and therefore something to be feared and shunned. As well as the singing of hymns much of the teaching of the church was focused on these beliefs. As a child I believed what I was taught and tried to practice it but this was very difficult and perhaps not surprisingly led to me suffering depression in my adult life.

*Finding the Taize Community*

One of the first things that began to help me to reorientate myself with darkness was going to the Taize Community in France where there was no mention of the devil. But many of the chants that were sung embraced the presence of darkness alongside the hope of light. One of them went like this:

> *Within our darkest night you kindle a fire that never dies away, never dies away.*

This would be sung many times and brought me comfort and hope that there was a fire of love in my darkest places.

## Coming to Quakers

Coming to Quakers also helped. I remember a piece of very helpful ministry that a Friend gave at a Quaker Life Representative Council that I wrote down and have stuck to my computer screen. It goes as follows:

> *The light is there even if you cannot see it*
> *The light is there even if you cannot feel it*
> *The light is there and loves you very deeply no matter what.*

Quaker Faith and Practice also has some passages that are very helpful in this area. In particular the vision that George Fox had when he was inwardly suffering. He says that he saw that there was an ocean of darkness and death, but also an infinite ocean of light and love, which flowed over the ocean of darkness.

> *"And in that also I saw the infinite love of God; and I had great openings"*

QF&P 19.03[1].

So again this idea that darkness and light can co exist but the light which is the infinite love of God surrounds and flows over the ocean of darkness.

## The Budhist practice of Tonglen

---

[1]     https://qfp.quaker.org.uk/passage/19-03/

Another thing that has helped me to embrace the darkness as well as the light is a Buddhist practice called Tonglen. In some forms of meditation we are taught that when we are feeling troubled we breathe in peace, for example, and breathe out fear. However, the Tonglen practice does it the other way round. So if we are feeling fear and anxiety we breathe these in, acknowledging them in ourselves and others; and breath out peace for ourselves and others. It sounds counter intuitive but seems to work when I seek to practice it in my own life, and I have written a poem about it called *'Embracing the Darkness'* ;

*I breathe in my bitterness, I breathe out my sweetness*
*I breathe in enviousness, I breathe out contentment*
*I breathe in my angry energy, I breathe out my loving energy*
*As I embrace the darkness I see glimmers of light.*

*I breathe in feelings of incompetence, I breathe out feelings of competence*
*I breathe in feeling inferior, I breathe out feeling equal*
*I breathe in my jealousy, I breathe out acceptance of my circumstances*
*As I embrace the darkness I see glimmers of light.*

*I breathe in my internal saboteur, I breathe out my internal encourager*
*I breathe in my sadness, I breathe out my joy*
*I breathe in my anxiety, I breathe out calm*
*As I embrace the darkness I see glimmers of light.*

*I breathe in my hatred, I breathe out my love*
*I breathe in my darkness, I breathe out the light*
*I breathe in my self doubt, I breathe out my self belief*
*As I embrace the darkness I see glimmers of light.*

*I breathe in my ambivalence, I breathe out my enthusiasm*
*I breathe in merely existing, I breathe out a thriving life*
*I breathe in my emptiness, I breathe out my fullness*
*As I embrace the darkness I see glimmers of light.*

*I breathe in my despair, I breathe out my hope*
*I breathe in my suspiciousness, I breathe out my trust*
*I breathe in my underminer, I breathe out my affirmer*
*As I embrace the darkness I see glimmers of light.*

*I breathe in my tension, I breathe out relaxation*
*I breathe in my hardness of heart, I breathe out a softening of heart*
*I breathe in my harshness, I breathe out my tenderness*
*As I embrace the darkness I see glimmers of light.*

*I breathe in my numbness, I breathe out my feeling*
*I breathe in my resistance, I breathe out my acceptance*
*I breathe in my loneliness, I breathe out my connectedness*
*As I gaze at the darkness, I see pools of light everywhere.*

I fear that might be letting you have too much insight into my soul but I felt it was important to share, as it honours darkness as well as light. It reminds me of Isaac Penington writing about love embracing all of us:

*"What is love? What shall I say of it, or how shall I in words express its nature? It is the sweetness of life; it is the sweet, tender, melting nature of God, flowing up through his seed of life into the creature, and of all things making the creature most like unto himself, both in nature and operation. It fulfils the law, it fulfils the gospel; it wraps up all in one, and brings forth all in the oneness. It excludes all evil out of the heart, it perfects all good in the heart. A touch of love doth this in measure; perfect love doth this in fullness".*

Quaker Faith & Practice 26.30[2]

## All in one and oneness, all for the divine

I think particularly this notion of wrapping up all in the one and bringing forth all in the oneness encourages us to embrace darkness and let it be transformed into light. I liken it to the natural world and the process of photosynthesis where trees take in our carbon dioxide and transform it into life giving oxygen; and in the process the trees grow, as do we when we honour our own light and darkness.

Another thing that has helped me in this area is a poem by Linda Rheuter[3] about giving all of ourselves to the divine:

---

2        https://qfp.quaker.org.uk/passage/26-30/
3        https://www.mindfulnessassociation.net/words-of-wonder/homecoming-linda-reuther/

*And the Great Mother said:*

*Come my child and give me all that you are.*
*I am not afraid of your strength and darkness, of your fear and pain.*
*Give me your tears. They will be my rushing rivers and roaring oceans.*
*Give me your rage. It will erupt into my molten volcanoes and rolling thunder.*
*Give me your tired spirit. I will lay it to rest in my soft meadows.*
*Give me your hopes and dreams. I will plant a field of sunflowers and arch*
*rainbows in the sky.*
*You are not too much for me. My arms and heart welcome your true fullness.*
*There is room in my world for all of you, all that you are.*
*I will cradle you in the boughs of my ancient redwoods and the valleys of my*
*gentle rolling hills.*
*My soft winds will sing you lullabies and soothe your burdened heart.*
*Release your deep pain.*
*You are not alone and you have never been alone.*

# Mark's Dark and Light: discovering balance and possibilities

I'm going to start with a letter to the 'broken' twenty-year-old me by way of introducing myself today:

> *"You're going to have an accompanier in your life marked by episodes*
> *and cycles. Sometimes it will be unlimited energy, and at other times*
> *energy will be only a memory. You'll live, love and suffer in both the*
> *dark and the light, low and high, happy and sad but like everyone you*
> *will live on the border. From low to high, back and forth, the bounds*
> *of the space in which you live will be wide. Like most people you will*
> *live in the shadow of loss. All will not always be what it appears at*
> *first sight. Sometimes you will lose your balance, but you will learn to*
> *be versatile and resilient, and to rebuild. You will need help, but you*
> *will also give it in countless ways. There will be hands to catch you*
> *and help you be yourself. Possibilities will arise and even when unclear,*
> *ways will open. You will live with paradoxes and tensions. Your*
> *difficulties will sharpen your radical edge. It's going to be tricky, but*
> *you will craft a worthy life."*

## Background

At first I felt some resistance to the idea of honouring dark and light. If I have a sense of regret about how my illness has affected my life then the tendency might be to 'forget' the dark and light, to erase them from my life story.

Although my first response was resistance, on reflection I value that the approach to the dark and light is 'honouring'. As difficult as it may have been initially, the title is a helpful framework for understanding aspects of mental illness - both as sufferers and as carers/family/friends. I see that honouring, and discovering, are methods and processes for understanding dark and light, and that honouring is a radical and healing approach to trauma. Balance and possibility are outcomes, the working through and out of experience. I'd like to use aspects of my experience and develop some of the ideas in the letter to myself, chiefly:

- We all live along a border of dark and light marked by episodes and cycles;
- Honouring experiences can be difficult yet helpful
- To promote balance we can all individually and as a community be a 'fulcrum';
- The experience of mental ill-health casts a different light on society and culture that can shape how we act in the world as Quakers;
- We should encourage kinder and creative language and models to understand the difficulties and trauma of mental ill-health and to promote recovery and flourishing

## We all live along a border of dark and light marked by episodes and cycles

I cannot say with any certainty that dark and light have distinct edges; I cannot say that they are cyclical, opposing or balancing. Our Quaker lives are shaped by and in the Light, both historically and theologically. My experience over the years is that we should try to decouple value judgments, and assumptions, about dark and light. One is not necessarily good, and the other bad; or not in ways we might assume. Light can be exposing and harsh. Darkness can be comforting and safe. I have known myself better and more equable in the darkness.

But, the reality of dark and light means the possibility of a 'border' or 'boundary' between them, between light, dark and 'us', and that requires us to understand the meaning and location of that border. And that opens up a way of seeing and thinking about balance and possibility. A 'border' offers an opportunity for encounter, exchange, porosity, resistance, closure and openness. Borders are strong or weak, policed, guarded, or crossable and amenable to redefinition and relocation. Some people live in a safe and certain place along the border of dark and light, others plunge across that border involuntarily. But we all live in relation to it. The 'border between' shapes who is in and who is out.

A border is also the place where difference and differentiation start (and meet) and become clearer. Where are the outer edges of darkness and light? What can people's experiences add to the wider social and cultural meaning of light and darkness, as people scope out the edges of experience and (perhaps) of norms and normativity? Experience of extremes can map out pastoral and spiritual boundaries and strategies, and the concept of borders can also have a role in defining and understanding community, of being inside and outside, included and excluded. Being distant from a perceived norm or centre is not necessarily a bad thing: it might call for social and cultural change. How much creativity, when looked at in context, is actually far beyond norms?

## Honouring experiences can be difficult yet helpful

As I mentioned, I had an initial resistance to 'honouring' the dark and light; my illness has created a weight of damage to me and to others, and the sense of loss and burden my illness has left me with is large. What is there to honour in pain, loss, hurt and damage, in extremes of experience and fear? What is the point and place of past experiences that are perhaps painful? Does honouring light and dark help to write the history of my life?

But as I worked through this I saw that at the heart of honouring is a key to remembering and narrating a past it would be preferable to forget, but in the forgetting would come distortion and a loss. Memory isn't history, and history isn't the future: recollection can be flawed, and my past is not a prediction of the future. I need to be reconciled with the reality of my past, not an imagined (or feared) version.

## How does honouring 'look'?

**Honouring the dark:** involves accepting the seen and unseen wounds and scars.

**Honouring the light:** is about accepting the gifts of hypercreativity.

**In honouring both dark and light** I acknowledge survivorship; I accept the gifts of love and care I have been shown; and I accept loss.

The keys for me in honouring my past are 'acknowledging and accepting' as the beginning of renewal, as part of a process of recovery based on three 'R's: Review, Rethink, Renew. The future and present need to be built on the reality of loss, pain, but also joy and love.

The challenge is not to be stuck in looking backwards, or locked into looking forward as a repetition of the past. 'Possibility' is the balm, the source of hope.

## To promote balance we can all, individually and as a community, be a 'fulcrum'

Accepting the possibility of balance immediately assumes (and needs) a fulcrum, a pivot point. We need therefore to seek and identify the fulcrum. The fulcrum can move or be in different forms at different times: hospital, medication, family, friends.

There are 2 parts to the fulcrum: what I do and what the community does. I have to

- accept that limitations are necessary for safety and flourishing.
- acknowledge the need to keep the destructive and disruptive at bay.
- accept the visions of 'the extremes' as frightening but also

as sightings of the horizon, of the edges and frontiers of my humanity.

That fulcrum creates connection and that creates connectivity: the fulcrum is always part of a wider structure/network of mutuality, community and responsibility. Looking at the fulcrum lifts my view beyond 'me' to a matrix, a network that includes the pivot point. Overlapping communities and networks of support can provide and sustain the fulcrum. We may individually or as a community find that we can be a fulcrum for someone; we are all part of a wider structure/ network of mutuality, community and responsibility.

What does a Quaker community do, and how is Quakerism helpful? Our central, core principles serve as a pivot around which spiritual (and life) experiences can freely and safely flow and fold into identity, without judgement, and be upheld by Light. Quaker ideas - and most importantly Quaker community - can anchor those dynamic processes of change, re-forming, and opening. Quakerism is blessed with a dynamic sense and articulation of meaning - meaning can change, develop, continually reveal deeper truths. Depth, interconnection and becoming are central to understanding our humanity and in this we are all a pivot point or fulcrum.

What is the relevance of my experience to the Quaker community as a whole? My illness has been folded into the life of my meeting not as a theme or as a problem, but as part of a patterning of care and compassion for myself and for others. My meeting, like my family and friends has lived through my episodes of up and down.

*The experience of mental ill-health casts a different light on society and culture that can shape how we act in the world as Quakers*

What did I mean in the letter to the younger me when I said 'Your difficulties will sharpen your radical edge'? I think this is where I have discovered the most possibilities and a sense of 'balance', where my Quaker values can be worked out. What can I do with personal and inseparable experience? Are there social and cultural implications to dark, light and balance?

As Friends we should acknowledge that there is a social and cultural dimension to our understanding of dark and light not only in terms of mental well-being, but in the wider understanding of our Quaker values and their place in our communities.

Light and dark cast society, culture, relationships, the world in different forms revealing the obscure and hidden (or evasive), fault lines, injustices, privilege, discrimination, but also positive alternative ways, values and routes. If you've spent time in psychiatric hospitals you will see how little valued they are in terms of resourcing, which says a great deal about discrimination and stigma on a societal and political level.

The most obvious possibility presented to me has been the scoping out a different form of life, of being radical because 'pushed out' of social and cultural norms and expectations. Success and failure can force us back onto our unseen strengths and that can challenge and unmask other forms of oppression and discrimination. A blemished career history can be a strong impetus to shape values that differ from apparent counsels of perfection (that themselves hide privilege and discrimination). 'Value and self-worth' defined by social conventions can be the most effective forms of oppression and discrimination, but also a route to transformation and prophetic living. We can advocate for the dignity of all forms of work and achievement; but our advocacy can be not only 'doing' but also 'being'. This latter can often be silent, but survivorship and being oneself can be powerful advocacy: I'm still here, and perhaps to your surprise I function normally. The advocacy of 'being' can be a significant challenge to people's assumptions and prejudices about mental ill-health.

Honouring dark and light also means a new set of values and metrics for life, for measuring and framing 'success', 'utility', 'outcomes'. Loss can push us to a more radical appreciation of ourselves, our lives, successes and failures. This process of looking more deeply at life's ups and downs could have radical social and cultural effects in terms of understanding values and the value of people and experiences.

*We should encourage kinder and creative language and models to understand the difficulties and trauma of mental ill-health and to promote recovery and flourishing*

19

Because I have lived dynamically on the border of dark and light, and have experienced loss and damage to my life, I have adopted this approach to each episode of high or low: Review, Rethink, Renew. Mental health catastrophes leave a trail of wreckage, and I myself have often felt that I have been gouged out and scarred by events. The language used in recovering experiences can be brutal - as I've said: catastrophe, wreckage, scarred. But I try to turn that into more creative, gentle and even artisanal: crafting a new life, shaping and moulding it from the injured and impaired.

I see a series of tensions:

1. Learning means looking hard at something I want behind me because it is damaged and ugly;
2. I don't want to be defined by an illness or my experience, but I sometime wish people could see the mental scars
3. Advocacy as 'doing' is not always more effective than the silent advocacy of 'being'.
4. Dark and Light do not have obvious values to everyone.

So what would I say now to that broken twenty-year-old, to hold out a realistic vision?

I would tell myself about the Japanese concept of *Kintsugi* (golden joinery) the art of repairing broken pottery with lacquer dusted or mixed with powdered gold, silver, or platinum. This idea treats breakage and repair as part of the history of an object, rather than something to disguise.

To the twenty-year-old me I say: you are a pilgrim and sojourner. Keep walking, sometimes joyfully, sometimes painfully, sometime in the Light and sometimes in the Dark. But Way will open.

# Chapter 3

## Mental health and wellbeing from birth

### Rosemary Roberts

*Does effective advocacy for mental health in the twenty-first century involve acknowledging the importance of the years from birth to three? In this chapter Rosemary outlines the evidence, and suggests many opportunities for parents, families and friends - and Quakers - to enjoy their time with the youngest children, laying solid foundations for their life-long mental health.*

## Crossing fingers doesn't work!

Around forty years ago I was teaching three to five year old children in a local authority nursery school. Children had to have turned three before they could start. One day in a GP's waiting room I saw a large poster showing a photograph of two teenagers with their backs to the camera, and behind their backs their fingers were crossed. The strap-line across the bottom read: "There are nineteen methods of contraception, and this is not one of them". And I remember thinking: "There are a hundred and one ways to help or hinder children's learning before they are three, and crossing our fingers is not one of *them* either".

## Why the first three years matter

A huge body of research since the 1990s[1] tells us that brain development in the first three years of life makes a lasting impact on children's futures. The quality of babies' and young children's attachment experiences - their relationships with people they see often, know well and to whom they are bound by love or affection – are thought to be the foundation for their later social, emotional and cognitive development. Babies' health and wellbeing from the start affects all their future outcomes. Research leaves us in no doubt of the importance of the earliest years from birth in terms of life-long mental health and wellbeing[2].

---

1       http://complexneeds.org.uk/modules/Module-1.1-Understanding-the-child-development-and-difficulties/D/downloads/m01p080d/david_et_al.pdf
2       Barlow, J and Svanberg, P.O. *Keeping The Baby in Mind: Infant Mental Health in Practice* Routledge 2009 https://www.amazon.co.uk/Keeping-Baby-Mind-Infant-Practice/dp/0415442982

In the long-running debate about the relative impact of nature (our DNA) versus nurture (learning and other environmental influences) on children's life chances, there is an acknowledgment of the limited sphere of influence that exists for nurture. Every child is *born* different, and since we cannot do anything about the 'nature' side of things (the genes with which a baby is born), our windows of opportunity to influence children's outcomes for good are necessarily restricted to the nurture side, however limited those opportunities might be. In other words, let's focus on things that we might be able to do something about.

The purpose of the research I undertook was to try to shed light on what these windows of opportunity might look like in the earliest years at home. In spite of the evidence there is still a long way to go in promoting the importance of homes, families and communities in the earliest years; and in developing suitable services to support families at this time. Findings from my study[3] inform the rest of this chapter.

# Windows of opportunity

The charity MIND[4] tells us there is a strong relationship between mental wellbeing and mental health. "If you experience low mental wellbeing over a long period of time, you are more likely to develop a mental health problem. If you already have a mental health problem, you're more likely to experience periods of low mental wellbeing than someone who hasn't. But that doesn't mean you won't have periods of good wellbeing" Here are four tips out of MIND's six tips for improving *adults'* mental wellbeing (the other two are about physical health, which is not a focus of this chapter):

- Try to relax and reduce stress
- Find ways to learn and be creative
- Spend time in nature
- Connect with others

It may seem strange to find information about adult mental health in this chapter about the early years; but these same factors apply from birth. However one of the challenges for us in thinking about our years from birth to three is that although we have all been there, most of us can remember very little of our own earliest experiences. So here are eight windows through which to look at life at home (and at Meeting); seen through an early childhood lens of

---

3        Roberts, R *The Development of Resilient Wellbeing from Birth to Three* University of Worcester in association with Coventry University 2007
https://eprints.worc.ac/511/1/Rosie_Roberts_complete_thesis.pdf
4        https://www.mind.org.uk/information-support/tips-for-everyday-living/wellbeing/

what matters for the mental health of babies and young children themselves.

## 1. Companionable caring

This is a kind of caring mindfulness, one of the greatest gifts we can give. All babies and young children delight in attention from their companions; the people they know and love best. Watching and listening companionably to a baby or young child is a way of paying attention that feeds babies' need to know that they are securely safe and loved. A toddler who seeks his mother's attention while she is washing up but is getting nowhere by just looking hopeful, might try hugging her knees. If that fails, maybe a little poking or dropping something on her toes will work. No good? Then maybe making a mess by tipping things onto the floor; or making the baby cry; or even picking up a sharp knife, or drawing on the walls. Of course, *then* there's trouble. It's usually not that he actually *wants* to do these things, it's because he really *needs* her, and knows that being 'naughty' *will* get her attention. Irritated or even angry attention from her usually feels better than being ignored. What such apparently 'bad' behaviour may actually be about is a real need for companionable attention.

If this sounds familiar, the good news is that it needn't be like this. Once small children have learned that we will, somehow, give them our attention when they need it, they don't seem to need it nearly so much. It is a kind of payback for giving children companionable attention as much as we can.

## 2. Our first language

We think of a baby's first language as the words they use when they start to talk, going from babbling through to learning how to express their feelings and ask for the things they want. Now that we have so many more languages and cultures all around us, does this cause problems for them with making new friends or settling down easily in day-care or school? Maybe a child's first language is Mandarin, Hindi, Spanish or English, but is it really the first? In reality, words are our second language, while every baby's very first language is a gloriously universal one: body language. Glorious because we all share it, and also because babies are born fluent! They are very attentive watchers of their companions' body language; and if we, their companions, are able to be as attentive as they are, we are all off to a flying start.

## 3. Playing

At the start, babies' favourite things to play with, their best 'toys', are us. As well as liking us being with them, they love it when we let them literally play with us, so that they can explore to their hearts' content. Our knuckles make such good teething rings, adults make much funnier noises than any rattle, and almost immediately babies learn that they can lead the way. For instance when they smile, we will smile back; and when they bang their hands, so (gently) do we. It is the baby who takes charge.

Slightly older children need to take charge even more. Their 'pretending' play is based on their experiences, pretending about things that they already know about. When they are pretending, children make up their own rules, so they are in control. And they choose what it's about and how it goes, that's not up to us. This kind of pretending play is essentially creative and profoundly satisfying, involving their ideas and feelings, coordination and thinking skills. It helps them to make sense of their family, their friends and their world.

## 4. Baby stress

There seems to be a prevailing myth that the lives of babies and young children are care-free, and that stress comes with adulthood. We call ourselves stressed when we are anxious, exhausted, fearful, frustrated, insecure, overwhelmed, misunderstood. Why we think that these conditions do not apply to babies and young children sometimes, is hard to understand.

Here are some of the realities. A baby who is left in the care of someone before really knowing them, may feel anxious, fearful, insecure and misunderstood. At the end of a long day most babies are exhausted, and sometimes feel overwhelmed. They experience the ebb and flow of normal daily stress, just as we do. What they most need at these times is promptly responsive loving or affectionate parents and carers.

Crying babies are never being naughty, they are signalling that something is wrong. But parents and other companions can't know from the start what a baby needs. Finding out can be a scary process of trial and error, especially to begin with. Paying companionable attention is the easiest and fastest way to start knowing what to do.

## 5. Belonging and behaviour

Very early on, babies and young children start to develop a sense of what sort of person they are. Perhaps they feel loveable, acceptable, enjoyable company even. How does this happen? It's a kind of mirroring process. When companions love them they will feel loveable. When companions accept them they will feel acceptable. When companions obviously enjoy being with them, they learn to see themselves as good company. Unfortunately the reverse is also true. But in every *companionable* moment they are learning to feel good about themselves. When this happens in the earliest years, an important and permanent foundation is being laid for life-long wellbeing. The warm welcome in Quaker Meetings can play a significant part in this process.

For all of us, there are questions about two sorts of self-concept, one sort leading to the other. First, as described above, is about how (unconsciously) we see ourselves; what kind of person we feel we are. And the second question, following on from the first, is about fitting in. Where and with whom do we belong?

This is about our sense of identity in relation to other people. How do we 'fit' with the people around us? What feels right? Who do we identify with? These are questions for young children too. As well as belonging in their family, in the normal course of events, the youngest children may spend time outside their close family circle, maybe with extended family and friends, in parks and playgrounds - and with Quaker families. This is how they begin to get a sense of what it feels like to belong; and perhaps what *not* belonging feels like too.

Behaviour goes hand in hand with belonging. It's like two sides of one coin. We might belong in a special friendship or with a partner, and those relationships come with boundaries and expectations about what kind of behaviours are acceptable, even if we don't talk about them. In families there will certainly be expectations about behaviour both for children and adults, although again they may not be explained. Day-care settings and schools come with rules about everyone's behaviour too. In order to be accepted and to carry on belonging we need to be aware of how to behave, and how *not* to behave. Belonging with someone, or belonging somewhere, means that our behaviour matters. Talking about this clearly and companionably is enormously helpful for young children.

A useful principle for life with young children, and maybe adults too, is: 'Say yes as often as you can; and when you say no, mean it'. Saying 'yes' often really is the key to saying 'no' successfully. Rigidly over-doing 'no' leads to a downward spiral of frustration, insecurity and shaky belonging (though on the fewer occasions when you *have* to say 'no' because it really matters, it's important to stick to it). Meanwhile saying 'yes' as often as possible leads to an upward spiral of satisfaction, security and belonging.

## 6. Learning

Sometimes people ask how we know when babies and young children are learning. They are never *not* learning! From Day One they never stop learning, in the same way that they never stop growing. But they may be learning things we would rather they didn't learn. They learn from everything that happens, not all good. If only we could turn off the learning switch until the end of this violent row or that frightening noise, but unfortunately there is no switch. Perhaps a slightly different question might be more useful. Instead of *"When are they learning?"* we might ask *"What are they learning?"* Babies and young children enjoy learning together companionably with their companions, an important way to start.

One thing to bear in mind is that young children - and indeed adults – tend to learn not so much from what we say, as from what we do. Children unconsciously absorb attitudes and behaviours from the people and situations around them, rather than as a result of being told things. For instance most parents want their children to grow up knowing about right and wrong, sometimes without realising that what they themselves and other carers *do* is a much more powerful influence on children than what they say.

We see them imitating all the time. Take saying 'no' for example. When we say 'no' as little as possible, but always mean it, we can be firm, but at the same time friendly and companionable about it. But 'no' doesn't work so well with children whose parents and carers often give in. When a parent or carer's 'no' hasn't worked, possibly the next step is threats, and if those don't work perhaps time out, and as a last resort, a smack. When this happens, children themselves will be learning to say 'no' that way too. This sort of embedded early learning, that ignoring and threatening or even hitting is alright if nothing else works, is unhelpful when they are young; and extremely concerning in older children and adults. Small children try very hard to be like the grown-ups that who are around them.

## 7. Helping

When small children help us, they get to learn about what grown-ups do. This matters a lot to them, because they want to be like us. We all learn in a kind of spiral and as time passes, with every new curve we revisit our previous learning at another level. As companions to babies and young children at the bottom of their learning spiral we are joining them in beginning to find out about their world, especially about the things in it that interest them most. Meanwhile, we are at the bottom of our spiral in learning about them, so it works for everyone.

From helping companions that they love to imitate, can come their desire to read and write like us, laying the foundations of their later more formalised understanding of mathematics, the sciences, geography and history, of all the arts. 'Helping' is a great way to learn about their family, their home and their world, linking naturally with the other most important way that they learn, by playing. Perhaps this is why short periods of gathered worship work so well with babies and young children – within their capacities they are helping with worship[5].

## 8. Children and the natural world

Many of us live in cities, in centrally heated homes, eating mainly processed food. Perhaps in seeing ourselves as separate from nature, maybe even in control of it, we are not helping our youngest children to experience the awe, wonder and fascination that is all around them. Going outside as often as possible really matters, even just around the corner or down the road. We can use all our senses not just to see but to listen, touch, smell and even taste (very cautiously, and depending on where you are) to explore and connect with nature. Young children delight in exploring this wonderful natural world into which they have been born. Small scale is best, with leaves, single flowers, tiny insects. With a magnifying glass or bug bottle in pocket or bag, going out can suddenly become a thrilling, magical, companionable experience.

Connecting with nature matters so much for children: for their curiosity, their belonging, their learning and their health. In sharing the delight, excitement and mystery of the natural world we live in, we can help them to see how much we depend on the living world of plants and creatures. Learning in childhood to care for nature can sow seeds of responsibility for the planet, so urgently needed now in the twenty-first century.

# Nurturing Quaker meetings

In the previous section 'Windows of opportunity', we have explored 'companionable caring'; 'our first language'; 'playing'; 'baby stress'; 'belonging and behaviour'; 'learning'; 'helping'; and 'children and the natural world'. Our early years windows connect with MIND's tips for adults in so many ways: 'trying to relax and reduce stress'; 'finding ways to learn and be creative'; 'spending time in nature'; and above all, 'connecting with others'.

This chapter is about the youngest children in our meetings. But we are

---

5      Quaker Faith and Practice, Children in meeting 2.74 – 2.76

enjoined to remember that each one of us - of whatever age – is unique, precious, a child of God. In identifying the youngest children's needs, and in emphasising the equal value of each person in the meeting, perhaps we have a call to action. Here are some questions that may help to nurture not only our children but everyone in our meetings:

1.      How can we make our meetings into welcoming communities in which each person is accepted and nurtured, and strangers are welcome?

2.      Do we cherish our friendships with children so that they grow in depth and understanding and mutual respect?

3.      Are we alert to discrimination against children and families on the basis of who or what they are, or because of their beliefs?

4.      Do we acknowledge that our responsibilities to children may involve us in taking unpopular stands?

5.      How do we help children to show a loving consideration for each other and for all creatures, and seek to maintain the beauty and variety of the world?

# Chapter 4

## Growing up Quaker

### Moya Barnett and Max Kirk

*In this chapter Moya and Mark describe their experiences of growing up Quaker, and the impact on their lives and mental health now. While these two accounts may be far from typical of the experiences of most children and young people belonging in our meetings now, they offer inspirational glimpses of what it can mean to be a young Quaker today.*

## Moya's story

I attended my first meeting as a two year old, with my dad in 2003. Of course, I don't remember this one, but I have early memories of playing under the table in the middle, performing plays in the children's meeting and of course all of the biscuits! But now my Quaker identity is much more of an inner one; like many young Quakers I have moved around a lot, to study, work and travel in different countries and cities, many of which didn't have a Meeting which I could attend. So, instead of one particular community, my Quakerism has become more focused on living a life which I feel is led by the spirit. For me, this means living simply, faith based activism and giving myself time and space for reflection and discernment in my daily life. I find, particularly when I am involved in more traumatic life events or activism, like working with refugees on the move, that my faith both gives me strength to act and gives me a space to let out the difficult emotions which arise from this type of work. A Belgian nun said to me after a period of silent worship together "We do what we can and the rest is on God."

Despite the Christian language and framework which I am now comfortable with, I am very confident that had I been raised in any other religion I would have become an atheist at an early age. As a Quaker child, my beliefs and thoughts were respected, no matter what they were, as they developed. I felt no need to react against Quakerism, because I wasn't experiencing a strong hierarchy or hypocrisy, both things I was reacting against in the rest of my life. As a teenager I memorised the entire communist manifesto to attempt to radicalise my rather unimpressed English class! What Quakerism offered me as a child was the chance to feel like an equal and have responsibilities, even just making the coffee after meeting. I felt respected as a person in a way which I didn't in the outside world, in which I was used to being talked down to or viewed as less intelligent because I was a child. Particularly there was involvement in business meetings. I remember one session we had in children's meeting when I was probably about 9 years old which was about what we should do with the meeting house. We made a mind map and later presented this in business meeting and our ideas were minuted and respected, a very novel feeling! I also did a clerking internship at Business meeting as a 13 year old, with another young Quaker, learning how to write agendas and take minutes. I enjoyed the work so much that I later accepted a nomination to be an Area Meeting co-clerk as an 18 year old. The internship helped me to feel valued and useful despite my age, and that was vitally important to my sense of self as a young teenager.

My parents chose to raise my brother and me in voluntary poverty. Our childhoods were filled with love and joy, but very little money, toys or TV. While poverty is a huge factor on anyone's mental health, I didn't find it a traumatic experience. This was because I knew that there was always food and shelter and because of the community we had around us. We spent a lot of time with other Quaker families, many of whom are still very close friends. They provided all of us, but particularly my parents, with a community and a support system. Moreover, we knew that my parents' decision to raise us in simplicity, to give to charity and to work less so that at least one of them was always around for us, was a faith led one.

When I was 9, my family moved to Zimbabwe. My father had a job at a Quaker training centre there, Hlekweni, which was supported by many local meetings around the country. The centre welcomed young people from the surrounding area to train them in practical skills, like plumbing and carpentry, as well as non violent conflict resolution. It was an inspirational project to be around as a child, with most of the village we lived in also made up of teachers and workers at the centre who believed in its non violent message and the opportunities it offered to disadvantaged young people. Their children were also a large demographic at the local primary school, Samathonga, which I attended with my brother. We were the only white children there, but despite our differences, friendships flourished. My brother played lots of football with the other children and I enjoyed looking after the younger ones and playing on the tyre swing.

Our school was definitely disadvantaged; the toilets were pits in the ground, which one of my daily chores was to clean by swilling a bucket of water around, and at one point the corrugated iron roof blew off. Truly living adventurously! Despite all of the material hardships though, I found when I returned to the UK, that the educational standard at Samathonga had been much higher than at my new British primary school. Living in Zimbabwe gave me an early understanding of solidarity. We had very little and those around us had even less, but there was a very strong community. Living out their faith in this way was not always easy for my parents, but this was never reflected onto me as a child. I was free of the burden of any of my parents' worries or stresses, which must have contributed to it being a positive experience for me. When we returned to the UK I went back to school and to 'normal' life, which I often felt dissatisfied with, feeling like I could be doing more, helping people more.

As a young queer pre-teen I was lucky enough to go to a secondary school which was fairly accepting, but even luckier to have had a childhood with older queer role models both in my Local meeting and my life outside. I could say I was lucky to have the self assurance to combat any discrimination that came my way, but I am sure that this wasn't luck. It was built up by a childhood of love, from my parents of course and from the community which I had at my Meeting. This is one thing that has stayed with me throughout my life, perhaps the best thing for my mental health; the knowledge that I am loved and accepted. Despite all of the difficult things which life throws at me, I have a solid and secure core which ensures that I can recover; and I have the confidence to leave or change bad situations without fear or uncertainty, knowing that I have a safety net.

Of course, I have had my struggles with my mental health, particularly in my teenage years. I was very frustrated at school, finding classes absurdly easy but socialising incredibly difficult. On reflection, the quality of the teaching at my school was actually quite high, but I was not stretched by the work, often bored and left to babysit my more challenging classmates. This made me hate lessons and I frequently ended up reading books under my desk to escape to a fantasy world, or simply not attending. Of course this didn't concern my teachers because I still got top marks, so clearly I was not struggling with anything ..........

Adding to that, as all teenagers do, I worried about my appearance, my body, and my social and love life. I can say without doubt that those years were the worst of my life so far and I wouldn't wish the experience on anyone. But throughout this time, Yorkshire Friends Holiday School was a light in the darkness, the highlight of my year. From the wacky games, to the dances, dressing up and general atmosphere of love and welcome, it was there that I felt accepted for who I was, not just by adults but by peers. I made real friends, many of whom I'm still close with today; and learnt to socialise, to dress (and to flirt!) in a non judgemental environment. Perhaps Holiday School didn't quite save my life, but it definitely gave me more joy than anything else I was experiencing at that time.

At my meeting I knew people who were open about their struggles with their mental health and saw how a non judgemental space was created for that openness. This couldn't fully negate the societal influence of shame about my own mental health struggles as a young teenager, but it certainly added to the welcoming feeling of meeting, a place I knew I could be fully myself, even when that was not my most happy, sociable or presentable self. I have often read and taken inspiration from Advices and Queries 10:

*"Come regularly to meeting for worship even when you are angry, depressed, tired or spiritually cold. In the silence ask for and accept the prayerful support of others joined with you in worship. Try to find a spiritual wholeness which encompasses suffering as well as thankfulness and joy. Prayer, springing from a deep place in the heart, may bring healing and unity as nothing else can. Let meeting for worship nourish your whole life."*

Throughout my life I have found that to be fully mentally healthy I also need to be spiritually fulfilled. This comes of course with attending meeting for worship, but also with living simply and being in solidarity with the marginalised and oppressed; to be open to leadings of the spirit, and to trust in the decision to follow those leadings, over economic stability. It also means having a community of religious or spiritual people around me, not just Quakers; many of my close friends are Muslims, Catholics and Jews. The depth of interfaith dialogue which I can have and the acceptance that the centering of God, or the spirit, in my life are incredibly valuable to me. I find that prayer, either in a formal group way, or informal more meditative solitary practice, grounds me and helps me to discern the way forward.

As a teenager, knowing I would be moving away from Sheffield and my local meeting, I applied for membership. Even when I couldn't attend meeting for an extended period (I lived first in the Welsh countryside and then in Italy) I still felt that Quakerism was an important part of my identity, and my membership gave me tangible proof. Later, when I moved back to the UK, I attended meetings across the country, rediscovering a spiritual home first at Sheffield Central Meeting and then at Milton Keynes Meeting.

My Quaker identity is strongly tied in with the help and support which Quakers gave me as a child and a deep desire to give back and be a present part of a community which is always there for me when I need it. While I am currently travelling around and don't have a local meeting, I know that I will search one out in the next place I settle; I can't feel properly at home somewhere unless I am attending a Quaker Meeting.

## Max's story

I guess you could say I 'grew up Quaker.' I have definitely said that before, particularly as a shorthand to communicate that I am not new to Quakerism when I visit new meetings. When I was two years old my parents came across Quaker meeting, and we started going most weeks. As far as I remember, me and my brothers were never forced or compelled to attend; it was as much up to us as it could be. There weren't many other children in our meeting until I was about fourteen, when we had a sudden influx of under-sevens and so the energy of our children's meeting shifted considerably: in response, I started volunteering with, rather than participating in, our children's meeting. From that point until I left for university, I attended almost every week.

I was accepted into membership when I turned 16. I went to Northern Young Friends' Summer Shindig (NYFSS), for five years, Yorkshire Friends Holiday School (YFHS) for eight, and Junior Yearly Meeting (JYM) for two, one of these as co-clerk. All of these choices were my own, which feels considerable; I am thankful to my parents for trusting me, for facilitating and emboldening me to make these decisions. I think that was huge for me, to have that freedom and choice both from my caregivers and also from the people at my meeting. I experienced no particular set of prescriptive religious beliefs, but a freedom to explore and decide for myself. I felt no agenda, just community and welcome and togetherness.

I have said before and will say again that being a Quaker – specifically, access to the Quaker youth residentials – changed and saved my life. It was at NYFSS one year that I first had a queer crush (of the big, all-consuming, classic sapphic teenager kind) and was able to talk about it (relatively) easily with my friends there. This was so drastically different from many people's first queer crush, at least then. (But really it was later, when one of my friends at YFHS accepted us, that I knowingly had a trans person in my life for the first time. And in that space, that person was happy and affirmed and loved.) It was escaping from my life and the gender crisis that consumed me into JYM arrangements committee meetings, testing out new versions of me, exploring the self that showed up there. It was trusting Quaker adults in my life with the new and fragile part of me that was questioning and exploring, that pulled me back, slowly, slowly, from a dark and dangerous place. It was being at JYM and being the kind of me I didn't know had so long been hidden, knowing I could not bear to hide myself ever again. It was going back to YFHS as my true self, getting years more there, aging out and hearing from others how I had grown into and beyond the spikey edges of my teenagehood, into happy and comfortable shapes of self.

Being a Quaker was also part of what inoculated me against accusations of weirdness: rather, I would turn such attempts at mockery into celebrations of my difference, and I still do. I was the only Quaker in my primary school, and one of a handful in my secondary school. Most of my non Quaker friends didn't know any other Quakers, and I grew used to this feeling. So, when I was also the first queer, and later trans, friend that most of my friends had, it was nothing new. Sometimes I felt weird even amongst other Quakers, especially earlier, which I would attribute now to a symptom of the unresolved sexuality and gender crises bubbling up to the surface, but that has lessened now. But I never felt a need to hide or deny who I was, and while this was not entirely down to Quakerism (some credit must go to my neurodivergence and my parents for loving me enduringly), certainly it was something that Quaker spaces fostered and encouraged in me by celebrating the person I was at every point, greeting me happily wherever I was.

In spite of all of the things I went through as an adolescent, I have remarkably okay mental health. There were certainly some dark years in my childhood and as a teenager; bouts of loneliness and bullying and love and angst that, with hindsight, could well have been bouts of something more serious. I don't know how I survived quite as (relatively) unscathed as I did, but being a Quaker was undeniably a factor. Being part of a community bigger than myself, meeting people like me (in the sense both of other young Quakers and of other queer and trans folks) was so crucial.

Learning to be still and quiet together is incredibly rare for many young people: a space that so easily facilitates reflection and introspection and regulation, both by oneself and in community. I don't know many people who had something like that as a kid – it's not available at school, or (often) at home, or clubs or (from my experience) in more prescriptive faiths – and I think it's a huge part of why/how I show up in the world, for myself and others. Quakerism was, and always will be, the first community, the first feeling of home outside of my house, the first found family I ever experienced. To get that, so young, is a rare and precious gift. I am thankful, deeply and often.

# Chapter 5

## Nurturing mental health
## in school communities

### Angela Greenwood

*Angela writes here as a Quaker with long experience of working in schools, often with the most traumatised and vulnerable children. From her perspective of the need for deep understanding and nurture, she advocates a relationship-based approach and offers a range of suggestions for ways of responding and staying calm.*

This chapter is for interested Quakers, Quaker parents, relatives and 'companionable carers' of children and young people; and for Quakers who work in schools, in child care or in any work with children and young people. It may also 'open some doors' for Quaker policy makers and trainers of school staff, who might share concerns in relation to the lack of training around work with vulnerable children and the fostering of mental health in schools. It is based on my book published in 2020[1].

The Quaker Testimony to Equality emphasises the fundamental right of each person to be treated with equal care and love'. We may therefore be concerned about declining school budgets squeezing out support workers for needy children, and teacher training which still doesn't include a module in understanding and responding thoughtfully to puzzling, hurting and challenging children and adolescents. The Testimony to Peace talks of avoiding behaviours designed to hurt, damage or provoke, which is laudable, but when children (and adults) harbour unprocessed trauma, neglect or abuse, they can too easily be pushed into such behaviours just to 'survive'. The Testimony to Truth encompasses integrity ... and authenticity. Sadly this was not the case for the young people in the Pupil Referral Unit where I worked, who often seemed like a 'bag of reactions' as they defensively bantered and provoked each other - just to stay on top. It was only when staff supervision and training there began to bear fruit that I saw the young people relaxing a little. They slowly began to feel heard and known and held in mind,open to conversations a little, and manageable learning.

---

1       GREENWOOD, A. *Understanding, Nurturing and Working Effectively with Vulnerable Children in Schools: 'Why can't you hear me?'* Routledge 2020

# Understanding and nurture

Disturbingly, mental health research shows one in six children aged 5-16 are likely to have a mental health problem, and 50% of all mental health problems start by the age of 14[2]. And The Guardian 8.6.23 cites 'record numbers of teachers in England quitting the profession in 2023'. Disturbing figures indeed. What do children need to grow into secure, thoughtful, resilient, curious, cooperative and fun-loving people? How could schools be preventive in relation to the mental health of children and young people? And in relation to staff too?

Let's begin with babies; what do babies need, and how can parents and those they are close to, nurture them?

In her recent book *'What Matters for Family Wellbeing?'*[3] Rosemary Roberts coins the term 'companionable caring' for the way the nurturing companions of babies and young children can attune and respond to their communications. Readers are alerted to babies' communications through body language, and their needs for connection and for attentive companions who also care for their *own* needs. These are things that I suggest school staff can helpfully bear in mind - seeing *behaviour as communication*: noticing and responding perhaps, to body language as well as words - and to what is *not* said.

The book moves on to how babies begin to get a sense of who they are, a sense of belonging initially to the family, and how, through love, acceptance and enjoyment of being together (including lots of 'saying yes', and only occasional firm 'saying no' when necessary) they tend to mirror the experiences they receive. This is not to say that parents and carers have to be perfect, just 'good enough'.

But vulnerable children have often missed out on this essential nurturing foundation. And although caring attentive school staff can make a big difference, the decrease in support staff and the increasing emphasis on targets and assessment of both staff and pupils, sadly works against it. Our most vulnerable and anxious children are frequently left unheard, and even excluded.

Increasingly, especially in inner city schools, classes include small numbers of students who just can't learn or respond to good teaching, sometimes evoking huge anxieties in staff, as their behaviour disrupts the concentration and the

---

2       Mental Health of Children and Young People in England: NHS digital 22 October 2020, and Wave 2 follow up 2021

3       ROBERTS, R. *What Matters? for Family Wellbeing: babies, young children and their companions' mental health and happiness* London: O Books 2024

learning of others; further burdening already pressured school staff.

Unexpected changes can be especially difficult, for looked-after children in particular. They have often experienced multiple traumatic losses as they move in and out of care situations. So for them, post-Covid anxieties, teacher absences, changes and transitions are *even more likely* to trigger traumatic memories.

It's not all bad news though. Difficulties can sometimes motivate the introduction of supportive systems and learning. One teacher shared how "our senior leader checks in with us regularly to see how we are doing personally, as well as how things are going in the classroom. She's allowed us time to focus on ourselves and the students we see daily, rather than the red tape aspects of education. This has allowed me to focus more on *connecting* with students, which is starting to pay off. I finally feel like I'm peeling away the levels of trauma, and enabling students to connect to the classroom."[4] Another school has introduced a weekly 'focus' meeting to update staff on happenings around vulnerable students. Our most vulnerable children, and teachers too, need to feel heard. Some children really *need* specialist services. But sometimes they are not available; or children are just too fearful and anxious to access them.

# A relationship-based approach

In my experience there is a lot that school staff and schools as a whole can do to ease these difficulties within their daily interactions and work with vulnerable children. With proper training and support, and thoughtful, committed understanding, pupils can be helped towards trust and self-acceptance; towards a capacity to talk through rather than act out; towards developing the secure base needed for learning: and towards accessing specialist therapeutic support.

My psychotherapy work at a Pupil Referral Unit (PRU) for several years took me on a huge learning curve. It was during this time that I saw first-hand the big difference *understanding* can make. Through training and work discussions, staff came to understand the effects of insecure attachment and trauma on the brain, on behaviour, on relating and on learning.

Staff also experienced how helpful clinical supervision and case discussions could be for those working 'at the coal face', both for themselves and for

---

4      *from: "Why so many teachers are leaving and others stay"* Jennifer Gonzalez in *Cult of Pedagogy* May 2022

the students in their care. Supervision can enable *staff* to feel heard and held in mind, as well as giving them a space to think together about the challenging children and young people they work with. As we talked through the sometimes puzzling and hurtful behaviors staff experienced, and the 'knee-jerk' reactivity the kids could evoke, they would become able to distance themselves a little from the stress and helplessness the children and young people 'put into them', and think together of more helpful responses.

We also saw how giving the students a 'second chance' experience of secure attachment, of being 'held in mind', of feeling 'heard' and nurtured, and supported through changes and transitions, could slowly shift their dysfunctional patterns, and enable openness to learning and relating - within the context of their increasingly trusted relationships. In the PRU we could *see* the difference these discussions, training sessions and reflections were making both for the children and the staff, and on the PRU ethos as a whole.

During those times exclusions slowly became a thing of the past, and the regular 'necessary' holding down of dysregulated children was reduced to almost nothing. The 'time out room' was well used though - when out of control children, accompanied by an understanding but silent adult, would go to calm down. We also saw how understanding, nurture and support could sometimes enable reluctant students to access the counselling and therapy on offer, and slowly develop the secure base needed for learning and functioning in society.

This experience led me to offer training to school staff in my local area. The training covered developing enough understanding of children's difficulties and their dysfunctional patterns and learning inhibitions, to enable staff to watch and listen to a child's behavioural communications and respond thoughtfully; and to talk through their concerns with others. The training covered both understanding and nurturing, and a relationship-based approach which they could use in the context of their work.

Crucially and in the long-term, such relationships can prevent mental health difficulties and psychosomatic problems later in life, as students develop the capacity to talk things through, to access the help they need, and 'normalise' rather than 'act out' (or 'act in') their 'buried' hurts and ongoing pain.

Government policy now encourages all schools to have a Mental Health Policy and a Mental Health Lead member of staff in post. Currently this is approaching 50% of schools. With basic training the Mental Health Lead role is to facilitate and encourage *everyone* in the school to be alert to any little changes in children in the course of their everyday roles, and report any concerns to their teachers or the appropriate person. This is certainly helpful, but does not in my view go far enough.

# Ways of responding

In school and in other social settings like Quaker Meetings a child or young person will naturally be drawn to chat to adults they like and feel they can trust. If you find a child or young person starts to share a concern with you, the recommended response is to listen quietly and in a caring thoughtful way. It is best not to offer suggestions or ask leading questions. Open ended wondering may be helpful as this does *not require* a response: "*I wonder what makes you think that*". It is better not to share your own 'similar' experiences, or even feel the need to 'fill' silences, as this can interfere with the young person's flow.

There are many things that teachers, family members, friends and Friends can do to support children and young people they are close to and care about - particularly when a child or young person seems to be struggling. Children and young people can face many challenges and will respond in many different ways. Sometimes when a child is really hurting they can need someone to blame and 'take it out on' for a while, to ease their pain. This can often be a parent or a relative, a teacher or a 'caring companion'. Although it can be difficult to bear, it can mean that you are trusted even in difficult and dark times to accept them anyway; without prematurely trying to make things better, giving them time perhaps to process a little and move forward.

We may notice little things which concern us, maybe behaviours or responses which are not typical. Depending on our relationship we may find opportunities to chat with them, or perhaps mention it to someone close to them. Talking things through with family members and trusted adults is the way many of us 'work through' difficulties.

Such difficulties may be passing or minor of course, but occasionally they may raise safeguarding concerns and we need to take these seriously at the same time as not over-reacting. Friends will know that meetings have safeguarding policies, safeguarding representatives and children's workers, all of whom should have done the Quaker Safeguarding Training. So if on reflection you feel that a conversation you have had might be raising a safeguarding issue, it is essential to take advice from your AM or LM Safeguarding Lead. And if a child or young person asks you to keep something secret, you need to say that you'll try to, but that if they're telling you about something that is hurting them or someone else, you do *have* to tell someone.

# Resources

Here are two films (Google to find them) that may be very helpful to Friends and to the education and parental world at large in understanding aspects of neurodiversity not uncommon among children. There are many such films and excellent and accessible resources available that may be needed at any time - a new puzzling child in the family/school/Quaker Meeting etc. - helping us to avoid being unnecessarily reactive, and showing how to be understanding, patient and nurturing.

*'Autism, a curious case of the human mind'* and *'Sensitive, the untold story'*

And here are two posters, obtainable in colour along with many others via my website[5]. The first offers reminders to remember and use thoughtful comments and gestures. The second is about staying calm

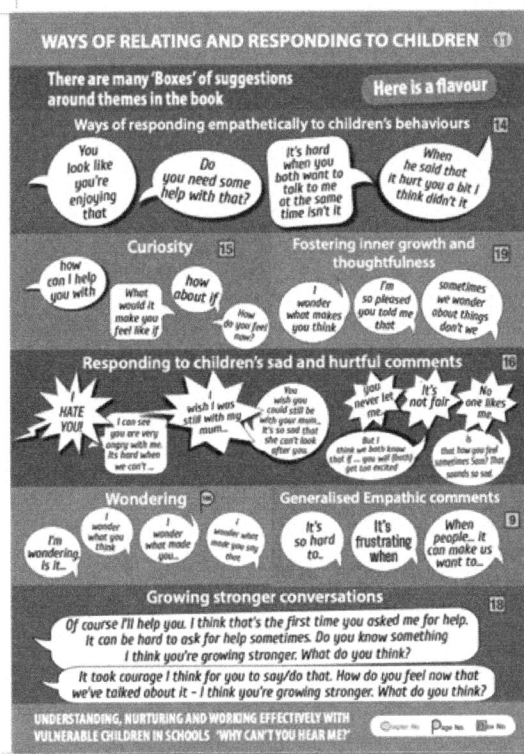

---

# Staying Calm

Quakers will be familiar with the use of silence and looking within to help us stay 'centred'.

A calm persona can make a huge difference. Here are some suggestions of ways to enable children to feel heard and held in mind, and to stay calm.

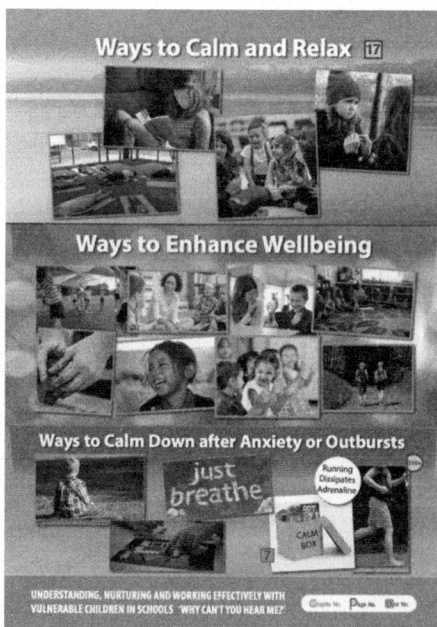

Find ways to calm and relax ourselves. Children and young people can learn to develop these too.

Mindfulness in schools can be helpful and is gaining popularity

Reading and slow art can be very relaxing.

Laughter and fun lift our spirits

Singing and rhythm can bring joy and togetherness

Being listened to and heard aids relationships and acceptance

Mediation (a Quaker 'forte') may be helpful to do and teach

Vulnerable children need time and help with calming down.

Silent availability without engaging is best

Movement allows adrenalin to be released

Many Quakers practice meditation or spiritual practices like the Experiment with Light. These can be particularly helpful in our relationships with our younger loved ones at difficult times. Going deeply into silent openness can often allow us to stop and keep a little distance in our interactions, and perhaps access much needed guidance. Such regular practices can also often facilitate present moment awareness, for example around not becoming too caught up with needing to help, or with our *own* conflicts around a particular caring relationship. Stopping, quiet attuned attention, or just leaving it for now, can also give much needed space.

But when the child is our own or someone very close to us, situations can be particularly difficult. It can be helpful in such cases to talk things through with a trusted friend, especially when this might involve acknowledging our own vulnerabilities. We can all of course 'grow' though these experiences.

# Chapter 6

## Mental health and youth work: navigating risk and resilience

### Jonathon Baynham

*This chapter, written by Quaker youth worker Jo, describes the current mental health crisis among young people, and how things have changed radically and rapidly in the last few years. The importance in youth work of balancing risk and resilience is emphasised, followed by the potentially disastrous effects of the internet and phone use on teenagers. How can parents and youth workers respond?*

Teenagers can very easily feel done-unto and talked about, rather than engaged with and heard. This feels at odds with our testimony to equality; and we need to resist this. We need to go carefully, to keep our commitment to plain speaking and non-violent language, and to remember that young Friends are Friends first and young second.

## The mental health crisis in young people, and what has changed

It is clear that something has changed fairly recently, for the worse. The evidence is clear. More young people in the UK are self-reporting about their poor mental health than ever. From around 2010 to 2019 anxiety, depression, self-harm and attempts (including successful attempts) of young people to end their own lives have more than doubled, and continue to rise with no signs of slowing down. Indeed growth in poor mental health in children and young people is beginning to look exponential.

Poor mental health is currently so severe in school that leaves of absence are commonplace, day-to-day occurrences for the young people I work with. When I was at school some twenty-five years ago, two young people in my year group were away sometimes for such reasons; now the young people in my youth group estimate the number to be between a third and half of their school year group.

We know that mental health, especially for teenagers, significantly depends on their feelings of belonging and wellbeing. We also know that in the longer-term, striving, failing and succeeding in supportive environments builds the resilience that is key for navigating the world. The best Quaker teen settings exist somewhere in the liminal space between *safe* and *brave*, whilst allowing teens to explore their faith in fervently non-credal, non-dogmatic spaces. As a youth worker I am mostly taken up with organizing and helping to deliver a wide variety of arrangements to enable the children and young people in my remit to spend time to do this. Underpinning this work is the need for connection, belonging, boundaries and faith exploration that is so essential to the healthy development of young people.

Below is a map of the ebbs and flows of youth work that I am involved in, that it is my responsibility to deliver. I do this with many different colleagues and groups of volunteers, supporting them with training as needed and helping to build the communities that children and young people need. Many report that it is the sense of belonging and acceptance that they get from gatherings and holiday schools that is so powerful in supporting their mental health through these difficult times.

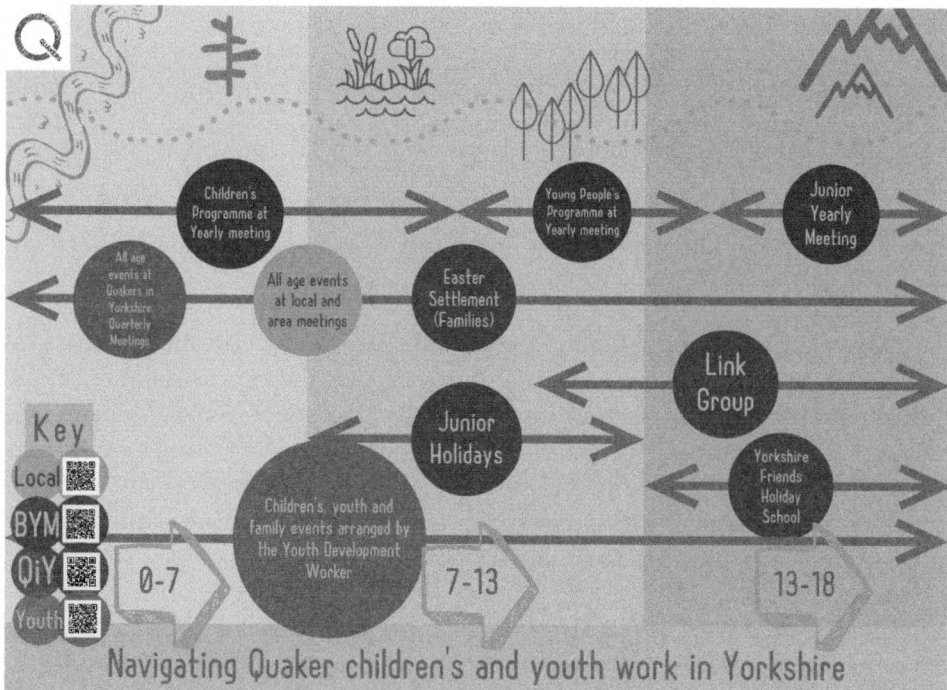

Navigating Quaker children's and youth work in Yorkshire

Much has changed in the lives of children in just a few generations. We've moved on from the 'seen and not heard' Victorian era, into a lengthier perception of adolescence that sells high fashion and cosmetics to 8 and 9 year old children and computer games to twenty-year-olds, to such an extent that both the child fashion industry and the computer games industry are now vital to our national economy. It is also worth noting the location of childhood has changed substantially, with the advent of internal combustion and locomotion. Extended families have become more mobile, transient and at the most basic level further apart, geographically, than they ever were before. My suspicion is that this distance, with the reducing number of trusted adult role models it entails, has had a very serious effect on family mental health. In my own family experience, I note the significant difference in family welfare (especially for my children) as a result of living on the Isle of Wight and on Lindisfarne. Either the prohibitively expensive ferry or the tidal causeway kept family away. Now, I live very near the A1M and M62 and within an hours range of perhaps 40% of our immediate family.

# Risky play and the development of resilience in childhood

For the remainder of this short chapter, I suggest that parental and societal attitudes to risk have a direct relationship to the mental health outcomes of children and young people. The well-known American psychologist Carol Dweck explains that it doesn't help a child to tackle a difficult task if they succeed constantly on an easy one. It doesn't teach them to persist in the face of obstacles, if obstacles are always eliminated. We see this philosophy play out in the construction of perfectly level, low difficulty, impact-resisting playgrounds along with issuing safety equipment to young people undertaking higher risk activities. When auditing a woodland alternative learning setting a few years ago, I asked a worker why all the reception age child were wearing ill fitting hard hats and adult high visibility jackets. The evidence suggests ill-fitting safety gear increase accidents and injuries by impeding movement, and falsely increasing a sense of safety. The worker said, "it helps the parents feel okay about leaving their kids". In this example the parent's psychological safety was prioritised over the actual safety of the children.

The parent's role in and around challenge, striving, failing or succeeding, is not easy. A ten-year-old girl of my acquaintance is bright and blonde and is broadly loved by teachers for her temperament, intelligence and effort. "Such a pretty girl, such a clever girl," has been the background annotation to her childhood. Things came easily and naturally to the girl from early on, and with many people implying that her that these successes were due to her specialness, beauty and intelligence, it is hardly surprising that when harder tasks arose and failure became a concrete reality, her confidence was deeply affected. On one occasion after a challenging episode, her parents found her hitting herself in the head, repeating "stupid girl, stupid girl". In this example we see the precursors of self-harming behaviors.

# The effect of the internet and phone use on young people's mental health

Part of an uncomfortable irony as regards risk and resilience to children and young people is that whereas parental tolerance for physical risk has reduced significantly over the generations with its consequent ever-decreasing resilience, parental tolerance for online risk has been extraordinarily high, although almost certainly by accident and ignorance. It is commonplace now for a parent to deny a nine-year-old attending out of sight, unsupervised sport in an evening with friends, in favour of allowing several hours of ultra-violent, misogynistic, war simulation computer gaming with an unknown group of live users connected by headset, or hours of unsupervised social media scrolling which can oftentimes have similarly unhelpful content.

In the context of our peace testimony it would be understandable for Quakers to consider the simulation of violence in computer games to be the most problematic instance of internet stimulation commonly used by young people. But that is not the only problem.

## An epidemic of mental illness

In a recent and very helpful book[1], the social psychologist Jonathan Haidt puts forward four 'foundational' harms for teenagers from *excessive* use of smart phones. These surely resonate in a common-sense way with all we hear, read and observe:
- Social deprivation
- Sleep deprivation
- Attention fragmentation
- Addiction

## Self harm and suicide

A study published in the Journal of Pediatric Phychology in 2012 titled 'The Suicidal Feelings, Self-Injury, and Mobile Phone Use After Lights Out in Adolescents' reported that mobile phone use after lights out may be associated with poor mental health, suicidal feelings, and self-injury in both early and late adolescents. Twelve years down the line finds us with increasing concerns in this area too.

---

1        HAIDT, J. *The Anxious Generation: how the great re-wiring of childhood is causing an epidemic of mental illness* Penguin Books 2024

The statistics in Haidt's book in relation to increasing teenage self harm and suicide in the US are astonishing, for both girls and boys. One table (p.31) shows suicide rates for 10 – 14 year olds from 1992 to 2020 rose by 167% and 91% respectively.

## Pornography

I suggest that a variety of concerns including the *simulation* of sex in pornography, and the *simulation* of care, connection and intimacy in social media, are more subversive than war games, as they claim reality and authenticity. We know that the challenge of porn and social media is the tendency to push content to extremes. The problem is that the algorithms that set the presence and prominence of content, use views, reactions and comments on content to do so. This means that even sensible negative comments such as "this is disgusting you shouldn't watch it," or "this is fake news, this didn't actually happen you shouldn't watch it" promote and increase the prominence of the content. In this way the most extreme content creates its own market.

Social media companies like Snapchat (which is used almost exclusively by young people) allow the promotion of pornographic content. The following is taken from the Children's Commissioner report into pornography in 2022.[2]

> "We find that pornography exposure is widespread and normalised – to the extent that children cannot 'opt-out'. The average age at which children first see pornography is 13. By age nine, 10% had seen pornography, 27% had seen it by age 11 and half of children who had seen pornography had seen it by age 13…
>
> …Pornography is not confined to dedicated adult sites. We found that Twitter was the online platform where young people were most likely to have seen pornography. Fellow mainstream social networking platforms Instagram and Snapchat rank closely after dedicated pornography sites."

# How can parents and youth workers respond?

In a chapter titled 'What Parents Can Do Now'[3] Jonathan Haidt makes helpful suggestions in relation to phones and their use by children aged 0-5; 6-13; and 13-18. He writes that young people feeling useful and

---

2       https://www.childrenscommissioner.gov.uk/resource/a-lot-of-it-is-actually-just-abuse-young-people-and-pornography/
3       Ibid pp 267-288

connected to real-world communities is pivotal to their social and emotional development; and that it's important that adolescents take on some adult-level challenges and responsibilities. The following headings included in the 13-18s section of the chapter give a flavour:

- Increase their mobility
- Rely more on your teen at home
- Encourage your teen to find a part-time job
- Find ways for them to nurture and lead
- Bigger thrills in nature
- 

Many other youth workers also report their grave concerns about what seems to be children and young people's growing addiction to their phones. This dependence has happened so fast, and was further exacerbated by the Covid pandemic, during which their phones were the main way for them to maintain their connection to their friends and communities. At our residential events we take in and keep in boxes, all phones from the outset. By the end, around 90% of the young people are glad we had ... and 100% of youth workers and volunteers are too! But it is very hard for some. None-the-less, engagement, presence, joy and attention increase enormously.

As the corpus of evidence regarding the damage that handheld internet does to children and teens grows, parents and youth-workers have to work out where their responsibilities to children and young people begin and end; and what to do about technology that we have put in the hands of young people.

# Living adventurously

As regards physical safety in youthwork spaces, my feeling is that our tendency to make everything as soft, lovely and low risk as possible under the guise of inclusiveness, probably isn't serving us well. There is a balance to be struck between risk mitigation, and accident prevention and preparedness. We would do better to consider risk assessments as tools to do risky things well, rather than reasons not to do risky things. Also, being explicit about the benefits and risks of some activities tends to serve better than pretending that we can make all our environments totally safe.

Here are some words from a recent biking event information poster,

*"DANGEROUS? A bit... there will be a first aider and we'll be attentive to risk of feature vs ability; outdoor learning and risk goes hand in hand sometimes, don't be surprised if there's a graze or two".*

Perhaps there is an underlying element here about being Quaker. Do our meetings grow and thrive when they come across as bold places where people live adventurously? And perhaps not so much when basically the priority is safety? Our communities, with their boldness and vulnerability, are what we offer the world. A friend once said to me of my Quakerism, "sitting in silence with all of those people must be so lovely". I replied "No, it's one of the hardest, riskiest things I've ever done. It's also one of the best".

# Chapter 7

## Food and Flourishing: connected eating for Friends

### Lucy Aphramor

*Lucy brings a heady mix of complex ideas and interactions to these thoughts on mental health and eating, for Friends. From her perspective as a radical dietitian, she challenges so many of our assumptions about food; about our unhelpful propensity for binary thinking; and the many inequitable healthy eating messages with which we live now. The chapter continues with a wide range of suggestions about what Friends can do to ensure that our radical hospitality is inclusive.*

It just so happened that my recurring teaching engagement in Canada coincided with the Atlantic Friends Gathering, a self-catered residential event held in a coastal church camp. If I had been at home I'd have baked something: banana choc chip muffins (including some gluten-free vegan) and parkin perhaps; but in this case I turned up with a large quantity of spicy lentil soup and headed to the kitchen to place it among the gathering cornucopia of savoury dishes, puddings and cakes, breads, cheeses, salads, dips, fruits, crisps, drinks and more. I stayed around to help, stepping in as stage hand as Natalie, the 'Friend-in-charge-of-food', expertly choreographed the dance of food safety and emotional care. To this end she was generous, graciously enacting her appreciation by listening. She listened to details about a recipe's heritage, the significance of the type of flour used, the provenance of ingredients, dietary restrictions, the unique merits of a dish. She fielded moralising opinions on eating and health without endorsing judgement. She repeatedly met cooks who were concerned about their special contribution being undervalued, offering second helpings of attention to those who were hungry for recognition and, perhaps, in search of healing repair. Beyond ensuring hygiene and improving menu planning, a deeper task involved tending the rich mix of fear, pride, hurts, joy, and anxieties expressed through food and eating in what was a highly gendered vignette.

Writing about this now, it occurs to me that Natalie showed us how to be worshipful through food. Bringing food to share was part of the deal, so to speak; but she nevertheless understood it as profoundly inappropriate to reduce the receipt of home-cooked (or any) food to a transaction. She refused the social script that makes food a commodity and instead treated food-giving as a long memoried, relational process involving love and witness. The kitchen was alive with the truth that food is much more than nutrients.

In other words, **'food and eating serve many roles and meet many needs'** which is a phrase I use to summarise my theory of 'connected eating'.

# Reimagining food and eating through inter-connection

There's nothing new here of course, but it is a significant statement coming from a dietitian because it upends healthy eating messages that treat food as a nutrient container, reduce food's impact on wellbeing to nutrient profile, and completely ignore people's relationship with food. By plucking out nutrients, standard messages move us away from an understanding of food where its value exceeds its chemical composition and embraces hospitality, nurture, identity, ceremony, symbolism, and climate and health justice …….. for starters.

Sure, some people approach food as fuel and I'm not suggesting there's anything wrong in this. I'm highlighting my concern with the wider, collective impact of organising ideas about food and flourishing through a mindset that silos off, and devalues, the sacred, the seasons, emotions, awe. It is hard to make sense of experiences around food and body that are forged by trauma, scarcity, neglect, shame and ableism (discrimination and prejudice against people with disabilities, assuming that non-disabled people are superior). By treating the body as a machine running on calories it ignores the reality (according to biomedical data[1]) that taste preferences, conviviality (eating together), life circumstances, feelings, spiritual belonging, dieting history and more interact to influence metabolism and wellbeing.

Having isolated nutrients as north star also means over-riding or disregarding body signals. And body signals can be super useful in certain situations – such as when someone with a nut allergy really fancies peanut butter. But consistently navigating eating through body-mind split, and ignoring circumstances, can lead to a troubled relationship with food. More broadly, it doesn't serve personal or collective flourishing.

---

1        eg. https://www.washingtonpost.com/archive/lifestyle/wellness/1999/02/02/eat-drink-and-be-healthy/b5dd05d3-00c4-4c91-bccb-410850790f0e/; https://pmc.ncbi.nlm.nih.gov/articles/PMC3134210/; http://www.ashwell.uk.com/documents/2015%20Arens%20and%20Ashwell%20NHD.pdf; https://pmc.ncbi.nlm.nih.gov/articles/PMC4479362/.
Doucet-Battle, J. 2021. Sweetness in the Blood Race, Risk, and Type 2 Diabetes. US: University of Minnesota Press; Hatch, AR. 2016. Blood Sugar. Racial Pharmacology and Food Justice in Black America. US: University of Minnesota Press.

# The fall-out of binary thinking

The body/mind split is an example of binary thinking. Binary thinking is a way of ordering reality through unequal couplings such as mind/body; healthy/unhealthy; fit/unfit; thin/fat; male/female; white/black; straight/ queer and so on. The pairings are hierarchical, meaning that social power and moral worthiness are at stake.

At root, when we approach food – and indeed life and thinking -  through categories of healthy and unhealthy or good and bad, we are establishing inferiority and superiority. Binary thinking, also known as diet logic when applied to food, mobilises the impulse to judge the moral worth of the person eating the food against what we believe they *should* be eating. When the person we judge is ourselves, it compounds our suffering and isolation. A different path is to acknowledge we feel distress – which might be guilt, despair, anger – and that we are still ok. There is still that of God in us. We ate something we hadn't intended to. This could have been to manage or numb overwhelming emotion, to connect with our body, because of hunger, and many other reasons. We didn't poison the water supply or burn down an orphanage. How would you speak with a close friend who was in the same situation? Can you try this instead of berating yourself? In other words, accepting the reality that you are awash with painful feelings while simultaneously being kind and understanding.

Binary thinking primes us to be judgemental. Take 'simply' having a piece of cake at a birthday party. If eating cake makes it impossible to move on with your day without self-judgement, regret, or preoccupation, what happens if you reconsider the belief that 'cake = unhealthy = bad = I am a terrible person". What if cake = cake? What if our claim to full humanity is innate and cannot be altered by what we eat or what we weigh or how un/healthy we are?

If we have a strong response to what or how much someone else ate, and/or their size, what's going on for us? Noticing how we feel and being curious about this helps us become aware of the assumptions we hold; and helps us think twice before commenting. Unsolicited advice can be presumptive, confusing, unwelcome, not the stuff that fosters right relationship.

If on reflection we think a comment *could* be useful, is the would-be recipient interested in hearing what we want to share? Nurturing a culture of consent through all our inter-actions is integral to social justice and, I suggest, tackling rape culture. Social injustice and sexual violence strongly shape eating and (mental) wellbeing. As eating disorder specialists Levine and Smolak (1998)[2]

---

2        Levine M, Smolak L (1998). The Mass media and disordered eating. In: Vande-reycken W and Noordenbos G (eds). Prevention of Eating Disorders. The Athlone Press: London.

summarise, "we may feel more comfortable educating young girls about the perils of dieting than we are about trying to achieve social change necessary to reduce physical and sexual victimization ... yet perhaps the latter will be more effective than the former in reducing the incidence of eating disorders". Let's also remember that framing our urge to intervene as a 'concern about health', and somehow therefore a legitimate vigilantism, may cloud our analysis. There is a long history of privileged people invoking health or social benefit to justify interventions that maintain the status quo. Advices and Queries reminds us not to let the strength of our convictions betray us.

It's true that foods differ in how they influence our metabolism. That people are different sizes. And that the way food is produced has huge ramifications for all beings and the earth. It doesn't follow that a healthy/unhealthy logic is useful. In fact, if our goal is to prevent eating disorders, promote body respect and inclusion, foster a culture that supports eating for wellbeing, tackle gender stereotypes and address sexual violence, advance health justice, and ensure everyone has dignified access to meals, then we need to explore the impact of binary thinking and its labels.

## Making room for eaters and in/equity in healthy eating messages

Sometimes the healthiest food is the ultra-processed meal we received from the food bank - it's that or nothing. Some people's main concern is that food feels safe - because of experiences of eating disorders, allergy, neurodivergence, sensory issues, domestic violence, body shaming, hunger, forced migration and much more. Standard healthy eating messages miss all this. They therefore imply two things: firstly, that all that is needed for everyone to follow guidelines is willpower and education – ignoring chronic pain, illness, poverty, zero hours contracts, access to food shops, caring responsibilities and other limitations of time and physical, financial and emotional resources.

And secondly, standard healthy eating messages imply that advice is universal. Hence people try to follow guidelines even when it's inappropriate, because they feel guilty, or worry they are harming themselves, or fear they will be blamed for 'not trying'. But 'eat plenty of vegetables' isn't always appropriate with gut problems, for example. Low fat advice isn't helpful for people with a small appetite. The standard advice isn't universal. It's written to meet (or centre) the needs of a non-disabled, neurotypical, lactose tolerant (Anglo), elite, cis-male section of the population. In a systemic gaslighting (manipulating people into doubting their own reality), it's taught as value-free science that everyone can and should adhere to. This is a good example of oppression at work, as it shows how we can unwittingly reproduce beliefs that seem fair, but in fact lead to harm. What we are led to see as normal, neutral, right, and the only way to teach nutrition, leaves marginalised people excluded, confused, stigmatised, blamed, and shamed. Accepting the standard narrative takes us out of right relationship, and stops more life-affirming approaches being imagined or supported.

This is different from arguing wholesale against a role for vitamins or dietary modification. Omega-3 and vitamin D supplementation may be indicated in managing depression, for example, and paying attention to glycaemic index may help reduce headaches and support mood and energy regulation. There are ways of going about these changes that deepen disconnect; and other ways that approach wellbeing and dietary change through interconnection.

One last point, linked to interconnection, is that because nutrition guidelines erase society and history etc., they exaggerate the influence of nutrients on overall wellbeing. I mention this as it can be helpful to remember that non-food factors strongly influence metabolism when trying to make sense of our experiences, which matters to mental wellbeing personally and because it is relevant to working for social justice. Raised blood pressure through 'white coat syndrome' is an example many people are familiar with. While conditions like blood pressure, diabetes and heart disease *are* impacted by diet, they are also strongly impacted by trauma, disenfranchisement, air pollution, racism, classism, intergenerational transmission of harm (epigenetics). For example, over fifty years of research in the Whitehall Studies[3] demonstrates that class differences in rates of heart disease are not accounted for by differences in diet and can instead be explained by 'status syndrome' - the metabolic impact of being treated like a second class citizen. There is also a wealth of biomedical data[4] that links hypertension and racism through the metabolic pathway of living with oppression, rather than diet.

Phew! Now what? It can be unsettling the first time we come across a new take on dominant beliefs that hitherto seemed normal, natural, and right, and that we relied on and felt certain were useful and neutral. If this is your experience, can you stay curious? Can you notice and name feelings and identify thoughts? Does anything especially resonate, an 'aha!'? How about anger or confusion? Are there any surprises? Would you like to continue the process of learning or unleaning, with others?

---

3       Marmot, M. (2015) The health gap: the challenge of an unequal world, Lancet 2015; 386: 2442–44; Whitehall LSHTM. The Whitehall Study archive collection. London School of Hygiene & Tropical Medicine. https://www.lshtm.ac.uk/research/library-archive-open-research-services/archives/whitehall-study-archive-collection.
4       Krieger N, Sidney S. Racial discrimination and blood pressure: the CARDIA Study of young black and white adults. Am J Public Health. 1996 Oct;86(10):1370-8. doi: 10.2105/ajph.86.10.1370. PMID: 8876504; PMCID: PMC1380646.

# What can Friends do?

Here are some ways to apply these ideas about food and eating to support mental health among Friends.

## *Model Body Respect and Interrupt Body Shaming*

• Stop commenting on people's bodies! Comment on the weather, a programme you watched, how pleased you are to see someone, a colourful scarf, all of those things. And let's *normalise* not endorsing body commentary. (For sure, we can do as we wish with our own body, the point is that we don't moralise about bodies in general).

• Read up on why comments on people's weight are specifically pernicious.

• Language - fat activists ask us to use descriptive terms such as fat, thin, people in larger bodies, to replace the 'o words' of obesity and overweight. (NB As feminist thinkers point out, political correctness doesn't stop us from speaking as we want, it exposes the pretence in imagining that what we say is without consequence.[5]

• Learn and practise ways to interrupt prejudice against fat people without shaming the speaker.

• Ensure Meeting's picture books represent people of all shapes and sizes and do not body shame.

• How can you share these ideas with young people? Read how author and fat activist Kimberly Dark does this[6].

• Have chairs that are safe and comfortable for every body.

## *Ensure Radical Hospitality Is Inclusive*

• When providing standard tea, coffee, and milk, remember to include decaffeinated options, sugar, sweetener, milk suitable for vegan coeliacs.

---

5     See Cameron, D. In The Feminist Critique of Language. Routledge, 1998. p159
6     https://kimberlydark.medium.com/haha-youre-so-fat-anatomy-of-a-put-down-fd9e-dea2ec27

- Have you included biscuits for Friends who eat a vegan and gluten-free diet?

- Is everyone clear on Meeting policy on nuts?

- Provide calories per dish only on request, so that people who need to avoid seeing the figures are not put at risk.

- If you feel the urge to comment on what people are eating or drinking be curious about yourself. What's going on for you? Where does this come from?

## Disability inclusion

We discriminate against people with disabilities (ableism) whenever we attach moral worth to presumed health or fitness status, food, eating behaviour, body shape and physicality, neurotype and intellectual ability. Can you identify the deep assumptions in these throwaway comments about food: 'I know I shouldn't', 'It's ok for you, you burn it all off'? A congratulatory 'this looks so healthy!' contains the echo of its counter-statement, castigating someone for eating an 'unhealthy' food. This type of sentiment embeds binary oppression and its hierarchies that work to erroneously rank people with disabilities as inferior to non-disabled people. It also makes the space very unsafe for anyone with an eating disorder.

Our good intent, often based on oblivious unthinking, does not annul the harmful impact. But the fact that we caused harm doesn't mean we have to be hard on ourselves. It's more useful if we can own the error, acknowledge the harm, put it right, and move on with our lives. For many people this means learning to be compassionate with ourselves. It also means letting go of the idea that we have to be perfect to be worthy. The thing is, we are all inextricably linked to each other across time and space. It follows that as a white bodied British person there is no blameless place I can occupy. Even typing on this keyboard makes me complicit in others' exploitation. That doesn't neutralise the impact of any harm I may experience, or invalidate *my* suffering. But that doesn't make me a terrible person. It helps me let go of the myth of perfection and focus on right relationship: an ethic of care and repair. It means being gracious with ourselves and each other as we start to recognise and reckon with our culpability for harm, and as we seek to muddle through to establish new ways of speaking about food that nurture collective flourishing.

# Chapter 8

## Gardens and mental health

### Zillah Scott

*In this chapter Zillah writes about the benefits of gardening on health in general, and on mental health in particular. A fascinating history of gardening is followed by a well-referenced discussion of why gardens benefit our mental health. Since many Quaker Meeting Houses are set in beautiful gardens, we already have tools to enhance the mental health of those in our Meetings; to enjoy the spiritual aspects of our gardens; and to consider how we might share them with the wider community.*

At the beginning of her book about gardening and mental health, psychiatrist Sue Stuart-Smith explains the way in which she feels that gardening benefits her mental health. 'A garden gives you a protected physical space which helps increase your sense of mental space and it gives you quiet, so you can hear your own thoughts. The more you immerse yourself in working with your hands, the more free you are internally to sort feelings out and work them through. . . . At times like these, it feels as if along-side all the physical activity, I am also gardening my mind.'[1] Her thoughts echo what many of us have found about gardening – that it improves our mental wellbeing and that there is something valuable in the combination of being in a natural setting and the work that we can do there.

## Looking back

The benefits of gardening on health in general, and mental health in particular, have been known and utilised for centuries. From the Middle Ages, monastic infirmaries had gardens where patients could recuperate and heal. This was not just physical healing; at Geel in Flanders, from the thirteenth century, 'mentally distressed pilgrims' came to worship at the shrine of St Dympna. Local families welcomed these pilgrims into their homes and provided care that included working on the land. Traditionally the relationship between the resident families and the pilgrims was seen, not as one between the healers and the sick, but rather as a loving community. This healing community at Geel might be seen as an early example of a Therapeutic Community, similar to those land-based healing communities which emerged in the middle of the twentieth century. The way that the inhabitants of Geel and pilgrims to the shrine worked together demonstrates another element that can be of extraordinary benefit in the impact of gardening on mental health – the way that it encourages community and working together.[2]

---

1     Sue Stuart-Smith *The Well Gardened Mind*, London, 2020, p. 13
2     Sempik, J., Hine, R. and Wilcox, D. (eds.) *Green Care: A Conceptual Framework,*

The creation of The Retreat by William Tuke in 1796, following the death of a Friend in the York asylum, began a new way of thinking about people with severe mental health problems and the way that they were treated by the institutions in which they found themselves. Tuke was horrified by the appalling treatments and conditions he observed in the York asylum, and created The Retreat as an institution where patients could be cared for in a humane way. In contrast to asylums at the time, where restrain was the norm, patients were free to wander around the beautiful grounds of The Retreat. Meaningful work was an important part of the treatment regime, and gardening was an important part of the work the patients undertook. [3]

During the nineteenth century, ideas about people with mental health problems slowly began to change. The writings of the American physician Benjamin Rush, at the beginning of the nineteenth century, demonstrate the way that attitudes were changing. Whilst some of his ideas belonged to the era of thinking about mental health which was to be abandoned during the nineteenth century, for example he believed in the benefits of bloodletting and purges, he was ahead of his time in believing that patients should be humanely treated. Like Tuke he believed in the importance of activity for treating anxiety or depression. He found that 'above all agriculture often cured this disease... agitating the passions by alternate hope, fear, and enjoyment, and rendering bodily exercise or labour necessary... to produce the greatest benefit'.[4]

There was increasing use of gardens in prisons and psychiatric hospitals from the early nineteenth century. Whilst part of the motivation for providing gardens and expecting patients and prisoners to work in them was about the provision of food, there was a growing belief during the nineteenth century that meaningful activity, and especially horticultural or agricultural activities, had healing benefits for mental health patients. That these ideas were becoming part of main-stream thinking in asylums is seen in the writings of Daniel Hack Tuke, psychiatrist and great-grand-son of William Tuke. His publication *Chapters in the History of the Insane in the British Isles* in 1882 gives an extract from the Report of the Commissioners of the Scotch Board of Lunacy 1881. They wrote that 'It is impossible to dismiss the subject of asylum farms without some reference to the way in which they contribute to the mental health of the inmates by affording subjects of interest to many of them. . . . For one patient who will be stirred to rational reflection or conversation by such a thing as a picture, twenty of the ordinary inmates of asylums will be so stirred in connection with the prospects of the crops, the points of a horse, the illness of a cow, the lifting of the potatoes, the growth of the trees, the state of the fences or the sale of the pigs'.[5]

---

Loughborough, 2010, p. 13

3          Stuart-Smth, p. 13

4          Benjamin Rush *The Diseases of the Mind*, 1812, cited Sempik, Joe, Aldridge, Jo and Becker, Saul *Social and therapeutic horticulture: Evidence and messages from research*, Loughbrough, 2003

5          Cited Sempik, Hine and Wilcox, p. 15

During the twentieth century, those treating people with mental ill-health became increasingly interested in using gardening as a means of managing and improving a wide variety of conditions. At Craiglockhart War Hospital allotment gardening was a key part of the treatment of soldiers suffering from shell-shock during the First World War. During the second half of the twentieth century both practice and research into the explicit use of gardening to help people with mental health problems increased and developed. Gardening became part of Occupational Therapy as a means of treating mental health problems during the 1950s and 1960s. Therapeutic Communities established during the second half of the twentieth century were very often in rural settings and the benefits of nature and of working in gardens or farms were a focus of the work done for mental health. The development of the profession of Horticultural Therapist in the United States, and that of Social and Therapeutic Horticulture Practitioner in Britain has brought an increasing focus of research on the way that gardening can help a wide range of people.

In recent years the increasing popularity and success of Green Social Prescribing, where people can be prescribed participation in nature-based activities, including gardening, has brought the important role that gardening can play in supporting people's mental health to wider attention. At the same time there has been increasing awareness of the impact that the disconnection of large proportions of contemporary society from natural environments is having on our mental health, particularly in the loss of opportunities to recover from stress in the natural environment.

## Why do gardens benefit our mental health?

For centuries individuals have found that gardening is a restorative activity, and there is growing research evidence of 'the positive relationship between exposure to nature . . . and an individual's health'.[6] But we also need to consider why it is that this positive relationship exists. There are two main theoretical ideas that help us to think about this relationship.

Rachel and Stephen Kaplan, academic psychologists, undertook research about people's relationship with nature and developed a theory that nature is a restorative environment. They suggested that the power of nature to restore us comes from four actions. The first is Being Away, that we can escape from everyday life and experience a conceptual change. The second is Fascination, that nature abounds in things that hold our attention without effort, in contrast to the effortful attention that so many modern activities demand. Thirdly is the idea of Extent, that the physical environment of nature feels like being in another world. Finally Compatibility suggests that we have an affinity with the natural world, that it is an easy environment in which to be. The Kaplans suggested that these actions of nature on us bring about Attention Restoration that brings relief from everyday cares and burdensome

---

6          Ibid, p. 19

focus of attention on tasks. Although much of the Kaplan's work was focused on the wider natural environment, they considered that gardening and the 'nearby nature' of small urban green spaces were able to bring the same kind of benefits as more extensive natural environments.[7]

Whilst Kaplan and Kaplan's theory of Attention Restoration considered that the benefits of nature were cognitive and rational, other theorists have suggested that there is an evolutionary origin in our preference for natural landscapes. E O Wilson's Biophilia theory posited that our connection to nature is an innate and powerful instinct which has grown as part of our evolution as a species. Further, he suggested that connection to nature was a fundamental biological need of the human species.[8] Roger Ulrich conducted a series of experiments to test the idea that humans have an evolutionary preference for natural landscapes. He found that people recovered more quickly from stressful events, including surgery and psychological stress, when they had a view of a natural environment as opposed to a man-made one.[9]

Whether the underlying reason for the beneficial impact of nature on humans is cognitive or evolutionary, those researching that beneficial impact are concerned with the mechanism by which nature impacts our mental health. In 2004 the Health Council of the Netherlands found connection with nature 'improves health through encouraging physical exercise, facilitating social contact and providing opportunities for personal development.'[10] Social and Therapeutic Horticulture (STH) uses these mechanisms to provide care for a range of health and social conditions, including mental health problems, learning difficulties, physical rehabilitation and social exclusion. STH differs from people simply gardening to feel better, as a trained Practitioner Gardener works with clients or group members to help meet their needs, whether they are psychological, physical or social.

In 2000 a research project by Perrins-Margalis looked at the quality of life of those participating in an STH project and found seven themes which contributed to benefit the participants. The first two were aspects of the group development and support in the project: feelings of accomplishment from being part of a group working together and the shared experience of those who participated in the project. Individual benefits came from learning new activities, sensory experiences of the project, creative experiences which the project enabled, emotional experiences of participants – they found that gardening was fun and enjoyable; and finally, participants had reminiscent experiences – the rekindling of positive memories.[11]

---

7        Kaplan, R and Kaplan, S *The Experience of Nature*, Cambridge, 1989, pp. 164-73
8        Wilson, Edward, O, *Biophilia*, Cambridge, Massachusetts, and London, England, 1984
9        Sempik, Aldridge and Becker, *Social and therapeutic horticulture: Evidence and messages from research*, pp. 34-5
10      Cited Sempik, Hine and Wilcox, *Green Care: A Conceptual Framework*, p. 19
11      Cited Sempik, Aldridge and Becker, *Social and therapeutic horticulture: Evidence and messages from research*

Because STH works in a wide variety of ways, it can benefit individuals in many different ways. STH practitioners tend to see their work as being in three main areas – helping clients to be in a thriving natural environment, undertaking meaningful activity and working in a positive social environment.

Whilst the theoretical underpinnings of the benefit of a thriving natural environment come from ideas such as Attention Restoration or Biophilia, in practice STH practitioners find that the benefits of nature come from the beauty of the garden surroundings, from the provision of care to the environment, and from a non-judgemental, non-demanding, calming environment for learning and development.

The practitioner aims to build a positive social environment. A good STH project aims to be a place without the stigma of ill-health or disability, the client gardener or group member is seen in terms of what they can do, rather than as a person with a diagnosis. Social connections and friendships are fundamental aspects of STH projects. These projects try not to work following an interventionist model. In echoes of the idea of Presence Theory, where the focus of the care worker is on 'being there, being together, doing things together' and believing that all have the potential to improve their own lives, the STH Practitioner aims to build a mutually supportive group environment.[12]

Whilst a mutually supportive group environment can develop around many activities, gardening brings particular opportunities for discussion of and exploration of difficult subjects. The metaphors of gardening naturally bring up many areas for discussion and contemplation and allow difficult subjects to be approached obliquely, or to arise spontaneously as work in the garden progresses. From the death and rebirth suggested by composting, to the strength and resilience of tiny seedlings, or the consideration of the removal of unhelpful influences that weeding suggests, gardening activity overflows with thought-provoking metaphor.

It is one of the fundamental tenets of Occupational Therapy that meaningful occupation is beneficial to human health and wellbeing. STH allows a wide range of people, some of whom might have felt that they were unable to participate in meaningful activity, to undertake gardening activities. Here meditative activities can bring their benefits, people who spend a lot of their lives being cared for and feeling helpless can care for and help plants, or people can experience the satisfaction of learning a new skill or completing a necessary task.

---

12      Cited Sempik, Hine and Wilcox, *Green Care: A Conceptual Framework*, p. 77

# Possibilities for Quaker Meetings

Many Quaker Meeting Houses are set in beautiful gardens. Meetings might like to consider the ways in which their gardens could support the mental health of people who are part of their Meeting. Those with responsibility for those gardens might widen their remit to think about the benefits working in the garden might bring to Quakers, not just that they need to make sure that jobs are done and that the garden is cared for.

The age profile of many Meetings means that the Meeting House garden might have a particular role in the health of those connected with the Meeting. There are strong links between garden-based physical activity and mental and physical health in older people. Care and treatment for people with all forms of dementia is helped by STH – the progress of dementia has been seen to slow; and gardening may be protective against development of dementia. Meetings might consider whether a form of outreach for them might be allowing an STH practitioner to bring a group to the garden.

The possibility for using the Meeting House garden as a tool to enhance the mental health of those in the Meeting could bring wide benefits. Kaplan considered that there were three aspects of gardening satisfaction: *tangible benefits* (in this case that the Meeting House garden looks better); *primary garden experiences* (the physical experience of gardening, watching things grow and thrive, being outside brings benefit to those from the Meeting); and *sustained interest* (in which all those who come into contact with the Meeting House garden, whether working in it or enjoying its beauty, have the benefit of fascination and the relief it brings from effortful concentration).

Finally, Meetings might encourage all who worship there to enjoy the spiritual aspects of the garden. Research by Unruh in 1997 found that gardens were a place of spiritual expression characterised by appreciation of nature, wonderment, prayer, or communion with God, even by those who did not consider themselves to be religious. Gardening prompted 'reflections about oneself as a solitary being', 'reflections about the life cycle and one's place in it', and the idea of 'gardening as a spiritual expression of community'. A study of gardening projects for older people found that participants 'likened gardening to a prayer and spoke of it as a way of relating to God'. This was independent of education, socio-economic status, culture or background.[13] Several British Meeting House Gardens are registered as part of the Quiet Garden Movement. This is a network of gardens which aim to provide a place for 'prayer, contemplation, stillness and rest for the spiritual, mental and physical well-being of individuals, groups and communities'. This is a possibility that more Friends might consider as a way to bring the benefits of their Meeting House garden to the wider local community.

---

13      Cited Sempik, Aldridge and Becker, *Social and therapeutic horticulture: Evidence and messages from research*

## References and Further Reading

Kaplan, R and Kaplan, S The Experience of Nature, Cambridge, 1989

Sempik, J., Hine, R. and Wilcox, D. (eds.) *Green Care: A Conceptual Framework*, Loughborough, 2010

Sempik, Joe, Aldridge, Jo and Becker, Saul *Social and therapeutic horticulture: Evidence and messages from research*, Loughbrough, 2003

Stuart-Smith, Sue *The Well Gardened Mind*, London, 2020

Wilson, Edward, O, Biophilia, Cambridge, Massachusetts, and London, England, 1984

https://quietgarden.org/

# Chapter 9

## Supporting Friends living with dementia

### Sheila Preston and Eddy Knasel

*Beginning with some helpful definitions of dementia, this well-researched and wise chapter from Sheila and Eddie tells us about the importance of 'personhood'; about living well with dementia and the experiences of some Friends. Bringing the subject 'home' for us, it helps us with how we might make our meetings more dementia-friendly.*

## Dementia is not a new concern:

The old age of William Penn

> *"His memory was almost quite lost, and the use of his understanding suspended; so that he was not so conversable as formerly; and yet as near the Truth, in the love of it, as before... His mind was in an innocent state, as appeared by his very loving deportment to all that came near him: and that he still had a good sense of Truth was plain, by some very clear sentences he spoke in the Life and Power of Truth ... wherein we were greatly comforted"*

> **Quaker faith & practice 21.62**

> *"Dementia is a growing challenge. As the population ages and people live for longer it has become one of the most important health and care issues facing the world. In the UK it is estimated that around 900,000 people have Dementia"*

> **NHS England website**

## Dementia: what it is – and what it is not

Dementia is not simply a natural part of ageing; it occurs when the brain is affected by disease. However, like many disease processes, it is more prevalent in older age.

Dementia is an umbrella term for a group of clinical syndromes. In the UK, the most common forms include Alzheimer's disease (62%), Vascular dementia (17%), Mixed dementia, which is a combination of Alzheimer's disease and Vascular dementia (10%) and Dementia with Lewy bodies (5%). Individuals may have more than one disease process concurrently. All are progressive and currently incurable.

Dementia can be the cause of symptoms that may include memory loss; difficulties with thinking, problem-solving or language; changes in perception; emotions (moods) and behaviour. Usually, these changes are small to start with, but as the disease progresses, they can impact very negatively on daily life.

The clinical manifestations of each form of dementia can vary quite considerably from one person to another: this emphasises the importance of not making assumptions.

## What does dementia mean for Quaker Meetings?

Statistics suggest that 1 in every 14 people aged 65 in the UK is living with dementia. Given the age profile of Quakers in Britain, it follows that there is likely to be more than one Friend with a diagnosis of dementia in each of our Local Meetings, and probably a similar number of Friends caring for people with the disease. This poses significant challenges to our Meetings in terms of supporting those with dementia – and their caregivers who in a very real sense are also 'living with dementia'. And yet there is significant anecdotal evidence that few Meetings are well-equipped to respond to these challenges. A member of one of the early QVoMH study groups had this to say about how her parent was treated:

> *An Elder said 'She gives the same ministry every week – we should discourage her from coming to Meeting for Worship.'*

Others reported that Friends living with dementia sometimes lost contact with their Meetings.

*Most Friends who had known her gradually stopped visiting her. Her decline shocked them, touched a raw nerve: perhaps they did not know how to relate to her anymore?*

So, how do we ensure that our values of equality and truth are explored and examined when our Friends are no longer obviously able to speak from their own experience? How do we manage to balance the spiritual and practical needs of our wider Meeting while including the Friends living with dementia?

# 'Personhood'

If we start from the premise that 'There is that of God in everyone' as George Fox famously said, it brings our focus back to looking behind and beyond how someone might be presenting, to find the *Person* inside the illness. This is the concept of '*Personhood*'.

> *"A standing or status that is bestowed upon one human being, by others, in the context of relationship and social being. It implies recognition, respect and trust."*
>
> Tom Kitwood (1997)

The term 'Personhood' implies that the essential core of an individual with dementia remains. Personhood is individual and speaks to the person's culture, values, and interests from before they developed the disease. A focus on personhood means treating people living with dementia with dignity and respect, in a manner that supports their sense of self. It focuses on treating the person living with dementia as a person first and foremost.

## *Respecting 'Personhood'*

As dementia progresses, people may experience feelings such as incompetence, worthlessness, grief, and/or loss of control. It is important to support their personhood as much as possible. Here are some practical ways to do this:

- Focus on abilities rather than losses. Look beyond symptoms, changes in a person's capabilities, personality, mood, and behaviour.

- Avoid making assumptions. Acknowledge the person's emotions and, as much as possible, consult them about their wishes, preferences, and needs.

- Use person-centred language. Words are powerful, and they can influence our perceptions and behaviour. By being more conscious of the language we use, we can avoid causing our Friends or their caregivers more stress.

- Family members, friends and other caregivers play a pivotal and unique role by contributing personal knowledge to help preserve personhood in late dementia. In an important sense, relatives, and partners also 'live with dementia'.

# Living well with dementia

This will differ person to person; but it will mean continuing with interests, relationships, spirituality, general health, and wellbeing as much as possible and for as long as possible.

The Alzheimer's Society has an excellent publication, available from the NHS, called *'The Dementia Guide, Living well after your diagnosis'*. It has an informative section on support services for all ages. The Society also run a dementia support line – 0333 150 3456 – offering personalised information, support, and advice.

## *The Alzheimer's Society's five key messages*

The Alzheimer's Society is the UK's most prominent charity supporting those living with dementia. They promote five key messages about these diseases:

- Dementia is not a natural part of ageing.
- Dementia is caused by diseases of the brain.
- Dementia is not just about losing your memory
- There is more to the person than the dementia.
- It is possible to live well with dementia.

# The experience of some Friends

Members of QVoMH's dementia study group have found that supporting those living with dementia can be a testament to their faith.

> *"The journey of dementia is a spiritual journey."*

> *"When I feel inadequate and lost myself, I remain in the present moment no matter how fragile it feels. I feel that is a gift we can give and at those times we may feel the sacredness and preciousness of that moment."*

> *"Looking back, I know it was a relationship of equals. It wasn't about me caring for a friend who was a victim of illness and diminished by it… Our friendship was strengthened as we continued to accompany one another in the spirit. That is a precious gift."*

Friends pointed to ways forward, through respecting our insight that there is that of God in everyone.

> *"I will never know what was going through his mind, but I held on to the thought that deep within him there was something more than his thoughts, feelings, and physical body; there is our essence which survives, a feeling of love which would comfort him."*

> *"I always start from where they were, accepting the emotions, being quiet and calm in my heart – holding them in the light. It was all about hearing their story… "*

The group also shared testimonies from those living with dementia who valued the way they were supported.

> *"I hold in my heart the memory of getting very confused, and someone, recognising my distress, took both my hands and said: 'I know you are frightened, but you are here where you are supposed to be. You are safe and we love you."*

> *"Paring our relationship down to the essential of being together, without expectation or judgement, was surprisingly liberating. There was much joy in simply being together."*

*"The sense of being loved, respected, cared for, upheld, is always with me."*

# Towards more dementia friendly Quaker meetings

*How can we make the Meeting a community in which each person is accepted and nurtured, and strangers are welcomed? Seek to know one another in the things which are eternal, bear the burden of each other failings and pray for one another.*

**Advices & Queries 18**

*Challenges raised by Dementia, Quaker Worship, and how to support caregivers and the individual*

*When we cannot 'know one another' as we expect, all can become puzzled and disturbed. If people do not respond as we 'expect', this can cause anxiety, uncertainty and possibly avoidance, because we cannot make sense of the situation and are not sure what to do.*

**adapted from the Retreat Lecture 2014**

For all of us, it is our presence – being alongside one another – that is our essential gift to the meeting. A loving community will find ways to reassure, to empower, to hear, to hold, to care for and to be cared for by a Friend living with dementia.

At its best, Quaker worship does not need words, or thoughts – but openness and love. Try and meet through attending to feelings and needs rather than to information and reasoning.

If you are living directly with dementia, Quaker worship may be ideal for you. The silence may be healing and calming for you; you can be a valuable presence there. However, some people living with dementia may be anxious and worried and may struggle with silence. It is important to remember that many people living with dementia respond very well to familiar words, phrases, and music – 'rituals' that are absent from the Quaker way.

Encourage Friends to continue to have meaningful social interactions and participate in activities. Our sense of identity comes, in part, from our connections to others and the things we like to do. Maintaining these connections helps Friends preserve their sense of self and can offer welcome distraction from the stressful aspects of the illness

Some people may forget the conventions of Worship – when to speak, how long to speak for. If Worship is difficult for a Friend in your meeting, consider whether someone can agree to sit with them to support them and help them to feel safe. It may be helpful to remind the person who has a dementia diagnosis of how things usually happen and they may need frequent reminders. Maybe a shorter meeting for worship could be arranged, or Worship in the Friend's home?

Is the Friend no longer able to serve? Can he or she be supported in some way to continue, or are there other things that they might still be able to do. Some people want to be busy and to feel useful and some find this a burden.

Friends living with dementia are likely to have times of great frustration and despair; some people may sometimes express this through aggressive words or behaviour. Always consider the person who is living with dementia:

> *When words are strange or disturbing to you, try to sense where they come from…"*

**Advices & Queries 17**

# How dementia friendly is your Meeting?

Meetings are not support groups, but they can be a source of comfort and solace.

Everyone who is caring needs help and support. Some people simply ask that we hold them in the Light; others welcome practical help. Some people need space to talk. It can be hard to know what to do, and hard to try not to offer solutions. Take courage – a simple 'What do you need?' can be valuable. It may be hard to respond: it is important to be honest about our limits. It is important that a Quaker community knows and acknowledges what people are doing and does not forget the people who cannot come to meeting because they are busy caring.

The Altzheimer's Society offers this definition of a dementia friendly community:

*A dementia-friendly community is a city, town, or village where people with dementia are understood, respected and supported. In a dementia-friendly community people will be aware of and understand dementia, so that people with dementia can continue to live in the way they want to and in the community they choose.*

Here are some questions you might share with Friends to gauge how dementia friendly your Meeting is. (These questions are based on work carried out by Churches Together in Greater Bristol (CTGB)'s Dementia Aware Churches Group.)

## Buildings

*'… our meeting houses no less than our own homes deserve our care, attention and imaginative thought.'*

**From Quaker Faith & Practice 15.14**

What conversations have you had with those living with dementia and their carers about how welcoming and safe they find your Meeting House and about any changes that would help them?

- Are signs displayed on the doors they relate to, not next to them? At eye level and well lit. Are there signs at key decision points in the building?

- Are your toilets accessible and well signed? Does the colour of the sanitary ware contrast with the walls?

- Are floor surfaces flat, with a matt finish and not slippery? Are changes in level clearly marked?

- Is there a quiet, safe space for people who need to withdraw from Worship?

## *Pastoral care*

*'Loving care is not something that those sound in mind and body 'do' for others but a process that binds us together.'*

**from Quaker faith & practice 12.01**

How have you tackled the challenges of providing pastoral care to those living with dementia?

- Have those providing pastoral care received dementia awareness training?

- Do you have safeguarding guidelines in place for home visits to those living with dementia?

- How do you support the caregivers of people living with dementia?

- Do you know where to signpost and/or refer people for additional and expert information and support?

## *Meetings for Worship*

*'Friends meet together and know one another in that which is eternal, which was before the world was.'*

**Quaker faith & practice 2.35**

Have you talked to those living with dementia – and their families – about their experience of Worship and business meetings?

- Are your welcomers aware of how they can best support people living with dementia when welcoming them into the Meeting House?

- Are your Clerks and Elders sufficiently dementia aware to know how to include those with dementia in the discernment process in a meaningful way?

- Are your agenda sheets printed in a way that people living with dementia can use them?

- Have you planned any all-age sessions that involve both the young and the elderly?

## *Community*

> ... *'encourage Friends to take responsibility for their rightful place in the life of the community in which the meeting is situated.'*

**from Quaker faith & practice 12.12**

What relationship does your Meeting have with local dementia resources and activities?

- Do you know who your local community contacts on dementia are?

- Do you have a dementia advocate who acts as a point of contact within your meeting?

- Have you run a Dementia Friends session for your meeting?

- Is anyone in your meeting linked to a local dementia charity and/or other local groups for people living with dementia?

This chapter about Quakers supporting Friends living with dementia starts with a background section about dementia, moves on to examine the important concept of 'Personhood', and identifies what 'living well with dementia' means. Moving on to 'Towards more dementia friendly Quaker meetings', it has focused on Challenges raised by Dementia, Quaker Worship, and how to support caregivers and the individual living with dementia. Asking 'How dementia friendly is your Meeting', there are helpful questions grouped under Buildings, Pastoral Care, Meetings for Worship, and Community. We hope this chapter will be a positive inspiration and support for Friends as we strive to make our meetings more inclusive.

# References / Sources of help

**The Alzheimer's Society** has a huge inventory of support and can direct you to specific organisations that might be pertinent to your specific situation.

https://www.alzheimers.org.uk/

https://www.alzheimers.org.uk/get-support/publications-factsheets/the-dementia-guide

**Dementia UK**  https://www.dementiauk.org/

**Age UK**  https://www.ageuk.org.uk/information-advice/health-wellbeing/conditions-illnesses/dementia/

**Dementia in our Quaker Meetings**  https://www.quaker.org.uk/documents/dementia-in-meetings-06-2021

**Reference:** KITWOOD, T. *Dementia Reconsidered: The Person Comes First* OUP 1997

https://www.amazon.co.uk/Dementia-Reconsidered-Person-Rethinking-Ageing/dp/0335198554

**Writer & Dementia Activist Wendy Mitchell** has written moving personal accounts of living with Dementia.

- Someone I Used to Know (2018)

- What I Wish People Knew About Dementia (2022)

- How to live with the end in mind (2023)

https://www.theguardian.com/society/2024/feb/26/wendy-mitchell-obituary

# Chapter 10

## Mental Health and the Law:
## Things Should be Better

### Alison Mitchell

*In this chapter about mental health and the law, Alison takes us on a deeply thought-provoking exploration of some consequences of the law as it stands. We are invited to reflect on ways that things could be better: in relation to early intervention, to the impact of social factors, and to how mental health services respond. And we are challenged as to what our specifically Quaker response to such consequences might be, with the question: "What is our Quaker ministry on mental health?"*

If you have a serious physical illness, say cancer, you will be offered treatments, which you can refuse, to the point of death. If you have a serious mental illness, say schizophrenia, you will be offered treatments, which can, in certain circumstances, be given to you against your will. You can be detained in hospital and given medication, whatever your wishes.

Nearly all mental health care is given with consent. You will be offered whatever treatment or support is appropriate and/or available – medication, talking therapies, social support, group work, gardening therapy…whatever. You can agree or not – as you choose. But in some circumstances the state will intervene and impose treatment, using the Mental Health Act (1983). This happens following a clear process: your condition, and the risks to yourself and to other people, will be carefully assessed by separate, specially trained professionals; your detention will be reviewed; you will be able to appeal; your family will be consulted; you will be given information and offered advocacy – but the bottom line is that you can be detained and treated against your will.

There are clear reasons why this may happen. One reason is safety. A serious mental illness may disrupt the way you think, may detach you from reality; you may hear voices, perhaps telling you to harm other people; you may become disinhibited; you may become convinced that people are seeking to harm you. For a tiny minority of people this can lead to violence; loved ones or supporters or strangers may be at risk; sometimes the law is used to impose treatment to manage risks to other people. If Valdo Calacone had been detained and treated compulsorily, he would not have killed three people in Nottingham in 2023. But we have a criminal justice system; if someone harms another person should they not be dealt with by that system? And if someone has not harmed another yet, but is felt to be at risk of doing so, are we incarcerating them on grounds of suspicion?

The other reason why treatment for mental illness can be imposed is when it is felt to be in someone's best interests. Mental illness can be fatal: perhaps through suicide or impulsive actions or maybe self-neglect or restricted diet to life threatening levels. Treatment can address these concerns. The treatment might relieve distress, might enable you to function as you would wish, might help you to reshape your life, might save your life. Does imposing treatment undermine the right to self-determination, the human rights of people who are compulsorily treated? There is a strong tradition of paternalism within the mental health system; if you're really ill you are not trusted to make decisions about treatment for yourself.

# Omar

Let me tell you about Omar[1]. He is an intelligent, smartly dressed, devout and polite man in his 40s. Sometimes he hears voices telling him that other people are out to get him. He becomes convinced that food is poisoned, so he doesn't eat. He's not sure about the water, so he doesn't wash. He doesn't dare to sleep for fear of what might happen to him. When he goes out, he feels that he is being followed and can be threatening and abusive to anyone he meets. He has been violent towards the people he knows – neighbours, family, friends, people at the mosque. He feels threatened by staff who try to visit him at home, so they are at particular risk. Omar has narrowly avoided prosecution for this behaviour. He has been compulsorily admitted to hospital many times and given medication, which he does not want. The medication works. Within a few weeks the intensity of his fear reduces and within a few months the voices subside to a soft hum that he can ignore; he eats and sleeps well; he looks after his appearance; he relates well to other people.

Omar's doctors diagnose him with paranoid schizophrenia. The diagnosis is based on the signs and symptoms that Omar describes and which are reported by those who know him. Omar's symptoms respond to anti-psychotic medication, confirming the diagnosis. Omar does not agree. He is clear that when he is in distress this is because a djinn (an evil spirit) has possessed him. He believes that if he can pray enough, he can control the djinn. When treated in hospital he realises he isn't as distressed and partially accepts that this might be due to the medication, so he agrees to continue taking it when he goes home; he genuinely intends to do so.

---

1     *Names and identifying details have been changed.*

Omar leaves hospital; he takes his medication and feels well. The medication makes him feel a bit sleepy; he struggles to concentrate. This may be his illness, but Omar blames it on the medication. He is prescribed a monthly injection of long-acting anti-psychotic medication and daily tablets. He stops taking the tablets first, but is still persuaded by staff to take the injections; after a few months he stops that too. The voices slowly return. Omar prays hard and struggles to control the djinn, but things deteriorate. The risks to Omar's health and safety and the safety of other people rise. He is admitted to hospital, always against his will, always under a section of the Mental Health Act. This has happened multiple times, but Omar has not accepted the doctors' interpretation: he is still just as adamant as ever that he is not ill and does not need to use medication.

Is it justified to ignore Omar's understanding of his situation? To impose a western, medical, interpretation of his experiences? That understanding works, in that when Omar is treated with medication his distress is manageable; he can function well; he is not a risk to himself or anyone else. Is it paternalistic, or simply a sign of a caring society, that Omar is given treatment which helps, even though he doesn't want it?

At the moment Omar is at home, still under a section of the Mental Health Act: a Community Treatment Order (CTO). Omar lives independently; his flat is immaculate; he visits his aunt; he has apologised to his neighbours. He attends the mosque and is part of the community there. He is taking his monthly injection of long-acting anti-psychotic medication. He doesn't want it, but feels he must take it because of the CTO. This can't compel him to take the medication, but a condition of the Order is that he attends monthly appointments with members of the Community Mental Health Team; they persuade Omar that he needs to take the injection. A CTO gives Omar's psychiatrist the power to recall him to hospital if he doesn't comply with the conditions; if Omar misses appointments he could be taken back to hospital swiftly. The CTO has been imposed because of the pattern of Omar recovering in hospital, but refusing medication when at home, leading to his mental health deteriorating, ultimately requiring readmission. It was assessed that imposing treatment in the community would give Omar the opportunity to stay well and to build a new life.

Objectively, Omar has a good quality of life while he is taking medication. His aunt feels he can become the man he really is. Staff discuss Omar's hopes with him, exploring work or study. His Iman tells Omar that using medication as well as prayer means he can be a truly devout Muslim. His neighbours appreciate the calm. Everyone's happy – apart from Omar. The staff supporting Omar are caring and respectful; they give him time and attention and listen to his views. Omar's detention, under the CTO and under the hospital sections, follows the law. Everything is done following strict procedures; all decisions are made in Omar's best interests. But Omar's narrative, his understanding of his experiences, is denied. The mental health system holds the power, and the medical model of illness is imposed on Omar. It could be argued that it is justified to impose treatment on Omar when he is posing a high risk to himself and to others. What about when he is not posing any risk? Is it enough to see the pattern of previous admissions and predict that this might prevent the next one?

# Maria

Maria[2] is currently in hospital for the first time, detained under a section. She is a slight, softly spoken young woman in her 20s. She did well at school and was aiming at a first-class degree. Five years ago, in her final year she left university and came home to her parents. Since then she has never worked; never travelled; never spent a night away from home. She stays in her bedroom, barely engaging with her parents and not at all outside the house. In recent months she only went out after dark, suggesting it would be harder to follow her then. She complained about the noise the neighbours made, saying she could hear them shouting about sex through the wall: the house is detached, and her parents did not report noise. Maria began waking screaming, saying she was being raped, when no one was in her room.

Maria's parents have persuaded her to see her GP twice over the years. She was prescribed anti-depressant medication and referred to the local Community Mental Health Team; she was offered a full assessment and invited to consider counselling. Maria rejected these suggestions and didn't take the medication. Recently Maria's parents became increasingly worried and again asked for help. When a Community Mental Health Nurse came to see Maria she was angry, shouting and started throwing things at him. She then turned on her parents, saying they had betrayed her, shouting and swearing. Maria was assessed under the Mental Health Act; the professionals felt that Maria was experiencing a serious mental illness and that she needed to be assessed in hospital.

Maria was very angry. She was disruptive on the ward. She talked about being attacked and raped. Two weeks have passed. Maria has been persuaded to take medication and she is calmer. She initially refused all contact from her parents, but now says she understands they were worried. She tells the doctors that her admission was unnecessary; she was stressed but is now well, and she should be discharged. She is clear she won't take any medication at home or

---

2    *Names and identifying details have been changed.*

see the Community Mental Health team, as she has no problems with her mental health.

The doctors suggest that Maria may have serious mental health problems. Maria won't talk about her thoughts or her emotions; she doesn't reveal anything about any threats she may feel or why she isolated herself for so long. The medical opinion is that Maria may have had psychotic experiences for many years with her thoughts and feelings becoming disrupted recently. It is also possible that she has a form of depression which has become more serious. Maria's mother speculates that her daughter's mood varies according to her menstrual cycle.

The one thing that is clear is that if Maria goes home, she will not cooperate with any ongoing assessment of her mental health, and will not take any treatment or engage with any support. So Maria is kept under section, in hospital, in order to receive assessment and treatment. The doctors talk about the 'right to treatment': the obligation of the state to intervene and relieve distress where possible. Maria talks about the infringement of her basic human right to liberty. Is it justified for Maria to be detained against her will when the risks she poses to others are minimal and she is clear that she does not accept the offers to manage any distress?

# A Quaker concern?

There is much to reflect on when we look at the state's power to detain and forcibly treat people – but is it a Quaker concern? There may be theological issues to explore within our concept of ourselves and our relationships to others. Is there a theological consideration of human rights? There are issues about liberty and human rights that could be explored. There is certainly the fact that some Quakers will be involved with the Mental Health Act – maybe as people detained, or as loved ones, or as professionals, or as Pastoral Carers when Friends in our meetings experience serious mental health problems. However, the key factor of concern to Friends is surely that **things should be better.**

# Things should be better: early intervention

The first theme to explore about how **things should be better** is about whether early intervention could have prevented Omar and Maria from becoming as distressed as they are. There is a lot of research looking at genetic causes of schizophrenia. And there are physical causes of psychosis: inflammation, pollution, brain injury, drugs for instance. There are also significant developmental risks. The impact of any difficulty on our mental wellbeing is different for each of us. It is helpful to see a mix of physical, developmental, psychological and social factors all influencing how we experience our mental health.

Omar has suffered significant trauma. His family sent him to the UK from Somalia to get a good education, but he felt abandoned. He lived with an uncle, who expected him to do housework and work in his shop without pay. School was hard: he was bullied and his dyslexia was not diagnosed. He ran away aged 16 and was street homeless.

Maria has never revealed why she left university. Maybe she began to experience psychotic suspicions and disordered thinking and became afraid of other people; maybe the pressure of exams and the weight of expectations was too much; maybe something happened. It is only speculation, but sexual assault can be a traumatic feature of campus life and Maria's allegations and nightmares were on this theme.

Omar struggles to form any close relationships. Is this linked to distress at his estrangement from his family? Maria is an only child, and her parents are very protective. Have they enabled her to avoid facing her issues?

If Omar had been able to access support to explore and address his experiences of trauma as a child maybe his experiences of life would be different. If Maria, and perhaps her parents, had felt able to use robust, assertive care when she first left university, perhaps she could have avoided years of isolation and distress.
What were Omar's and Maria's experiences of parenting, of attachment, of safety, of building relationships and a sense of self in their early years? Long term, bespoke, responsive care is not readily available. Preventative input is costly, and its success hard to validate.

## Things should be better: the impact of social factors

The second way in which **things should be better** is the impact of social factors. Omar is isolated: he occasionally sees one elderly aunt and has few social contacts. He has no meaningful work experience. He suffers racism every day. As a black Muslim man, he feels judged and stereotyped. He faces the stigma of being someone who uses mental health services. And that stigma contributed to Maria refusing to use services for so long.

Our mental health is affected by our living situation. Poverty, discrimination, inequality, lack of agency, lack of opportunity, isolation, despair, poor housing, poor education, lack of green space, climate change anxiety, our parents, their wellbeing and opportunities, the communities in which we grow up... Black men are four times more likely to be detained under the Mental Health Act than white men. A black man in distress may be perceived as dangerous, while a white woman in distress may be perceived as upset. The discrimination is not usually about racist assessments, but about why black men need to be detained. Their experience of the world leads them to distress and to illness: a racist system, and their lifelong experiences, may be as great a risk of developing schizophrenia as any genetic inheritance.

# Things should be better: how mental health services respond

Thirdly, **things should be better** in the way that our mental health services are able to respond. Some of us have supportive family or friends, or a faith community that can enable us to come through trauma. Some of us are offered robust professional support: family therapy; individual therapy; support to address early trauma; early intervention; assertive services – all these help. There are many committed, caring professionals working in mental health services – but not enough of them. There are unacceptable waiting lists of many months for an initial mental health assessment. Most people experiencing a mental health problem will only be offered medication, which can be a very helpful tool, if there is also support to explore why you are having problems. There are Early Intervention in Psychosis teams, offering intensive support; their excellent work is limited by the size of their workload. If you miss a couple of appointments anywhere in specialist mental health services, you are likely to be discharged; there's limited scope to explore why you didn't attend. You may look for support as you feel your grip on things faltering, but the services may be so stretched that there may be no response until you are in crisis.

Admission to hospital only happens as a last resort; never as a safe 'asylum'. Sometimes there are no vacant psychiatric hospital beds anywhere in the country. This means some people are discharged as soon as they settle a little, returning home without time to address what led to their admission. Others are placed in hospital hundreds of miles away from home. It means people in crisis have to wait: you may need a Mental Health Act assessment but because there is no bed available you may wait for days until the assessment and admission happens. Even the police are so stretched that they often won't carry out routine welfare checks.

Mental health services are in crisis. As I write, the government is working to reform the Mental Health Act in England and Wales (the law is Scotland is slightly different, but similar) which is welcome. But without radical reform of how services are designed and delivered, no significant change will be felt.

So, **things should be better.**
We live in a society that responds poorly to trauma, where inequality affects the mental health of everyone, and where mental health services are poorly funded and undervalued. Is this a Quaker concern?

**What is our Quaker ministry on mental health?**

*These links are to information about the Mental Health Act in England and Wales:*

*https://www.nhs.uk/mental-health/social-care-and-your-rights/mental-health-and-the-law/mental-health-act/*

*https://www.mind.org.uk/information-support/legal-rights/mental-health-act-1983/about-the-mha-1983/*

*This link is to information about the Scottish Mental Health Act:*
*https://www.mwcscot.org.uk/law-and-rights/mental-health-act*

# Chapter 11

## Quaker Voices on Mental Health Behind Bars

*Chapter 11 is a collaboration involving seven Quaker voices whose identities and locations are necessarily confidential. The seven voices are those of four prison residents and three prison chaplains who support them. The chapter is mainly conversations in response to a series of questions about mental health and the ways in which these prisoners are navigating custody at different stages of their sentences. It ends with an arrestingly powerful image.*

*This chapter focuses on aspects of mental health for those living inside the prison system. It is a collaboration between four residents and three chaplains who support them. They are part of Quaker communities in two different establishments in the male estate, one a category A high security prison and the other a Category B training and therapeutic prison. In both prisons the chaplains hold a weekly Quaker meeting supported by Friends from local meetings. In one, the meeting has been held for over 10 years. The other has been running since the 1980s. Both have around 8-10 attending and are open to any faith and none, with a few men choosing to identify as Quaker. Both meetings have a half hour of quiet, usually with a reading and spoken ministry, followed by time for fellowship and refreshments. The men enjoy talking to their Quaker visitors and Friends affirm that of God in their encounters with them. This is a tangible expression of fellowship in community which is vital for resilience and mental health inside mainstream prisons.*

*The multi-faith team of chaplains has a presence across the whole prison, aside from its function to lead worship for each faith group, so its influence is widespread. In custody religious identity has more personal value because other identities are taken away. Religious registration is a matter of personal choice. Some revert to the faith of their childhood; others use their time in custody for genuine exploration. In this context the radical, simple and spiritual values of Quakers are refreshingly open and non-judgemental. Many find acceptance in a safe and welcoming space, and deep peace in the stillness.*

*Quaker Prison Chaplains bring a mix of life experience with them into this ministry which often begins in a voluntary capacity and sometimes grows into contracted work. Chaplains have no specific training in mental health but these QPCs have worked as teachers and counsellors before they came into prison ministry.*
*The four residents who took part in this collaboration are all serving life or a lengthy sentence ranging from a minimum term of nine to twenty-five years. They came into custody as category A or B prisoners and will be required to demonstrate progress in*

*reducing their risks before they can be considered for release. We have tried to reference any relevant prison detail briefly but for more background information and up-to-date statistics about UK prisons, we encourage you to read the Bromley Briefings published annually by the Prison Reform Trust.[1]*

*Our contribution here is offered as a conversation in response to questions about mental health and the ways in which these prisoners are navigating custody at different stages of their sentence. We are not identifying ourselves, to comply with the code of conduct for our role in the prison service and to safeguard all of us. Importantly we do not wish to cause distress to any victim of their crimes or their families.*

*Our conversation starts with their current community and we asked how it demonstrates welcome and acceptance since these are fundamental to mental well-being. In the mainstream prison estate, individuals largely create their own community although there are many challenges.*

# How do community values in your prison promote mental well-being?

P: "There's a core of residents, mostly long-termers or Lifers who just want to get on with doing their time quietly without causing trouble. I count myself as one of this group and believe we are often a calming effect on the wing, in workshops and even at chaplaincy activities. There are problems with drugs, debt, bullying and other anti-social behaviours from some other groups. Officers here vary in attitude and sadly many of the experienced ones are leaving. Equality and diversity issues do sometimes arise and become problematic. Most inmates seem to accept others' individualities or keep their opinions to themselves."

D: "There are smaller communities within our prison aside from official groups and activities, which are more organic groups based on social values. What welcome, kindness or acceptance you meet is in part dependant on the attitude you take but more so on which labels come with your offence. There is an initial tension between main-stream and support wings (those for vulnerable prisoners) but this starts to subside with time shared together, as in chaplaincy groups. Kindness and acceptance are often like mirrors – the more you reflect towards others, the more you get back in return (usually)."

S: "I am part of a Therapeutic Community, which encourages residents to live together and accept each other for who they are, not based on their crime. We have a welcome cabinet for new residents to the wing. We also have two

---

1        https://prisonreformtrust.org.uk/project/prison-the-facts/

community meetings twice a week, where we can air our differences in a calm and respectful way."

R: "I am also part of a Therapeutic Community which is welcoming and friendly - very different from my experience of mainstream prisons. Here relationships are looked at in detail and there is a lot of emphasis placed on valuing yourself and others equally. Behaviours and thinking that diverge from this expectation are challenged by the residents and explored in depth within therapeutic groups.

This kind of work can be very emotional for an individual who will be asked to expose core value systems and defensive strategies which we have each evolved to cope with painful experiences of loss or childhood trauma. Each community within the Therapeutic Community has a its own constitution written by the community which promotes acceptance, boundaries and trust so that every individual can be respected and their voice acknowledged.

I have found other mainstream establishments I've been in over the past 30 years make attempts to care for the individual but don't have the resources to match their expectation. All prisons offer support from Chaplaincy, Safer Custody, mental health and drug workers, Listeners and Samaritans by phone.

The difficulty with mental health issues is that although help may be available, the person in need can be locked in old patterns of thinking and behaviour that do not recognise support and see asking for help as an admission that there is something wrong with them. There is a misconception that promotes the idea that vulnerability in prison will attract bullying and violence so people with mental health issues feel less inclined to speak about their problem for fears around their safety.

In Therapeutic Communities these issues are addressed head on and people are reassured that they are safe to be open about their fears and vulnerability. Understanding personal trauma or negative life experiences helps unpack the thoughts and emotions that are triggered when our brain filters information and makes links to past experiences we find difficult to cope with. By doing this we learn to manage our responses if we are mindful of the cycle that occurs in the present."

## What gives you a sense of belonging?

D: "I've been at my current prison for about 6 years. Belonging to different communities with different people, it's difficult not to wear different masks. What helps me feel part of these communities and not need a mask depends on the other people and this is always changing."

P: "I still don't feel a sense of belonging in prison but I do understand that I deserve to be here. I miss my family, my few close friends who have stuck by me. I also miss being loved, although I'm coping and I've accepted that I'll probably never rekindle any previous relationships. I keep busy with volunteer roles, a paid mentor job in education, studying for a degree, playing sport, doing art and music, going to chapel activities and singing in the choir.

S: "I've been at this prison coming up for 7 years. There was no sense of belonging at all at my previous establishment. You were left mostly on your own, with everyday looking over your shoulder. What helped me was staying on my own behind my door, with my own problems. Here, I do feel very much part of this Therapeutic Community. What helps me is that we challenge each other on our behaviours, we have mediation meetings between residents for those that don't get along. We can also call a special group meeting and ask our members for support and discuss with them what is going on for us."

R: "I do feel a sense of belonging at this Therapeutic Community but the necessity to isolate during Covid interrupted that feeling of connection. We've all had to adjust in our routines to re-engage face to face yet there is an underlying uneasiness that isolation could return, so what is the point of making all the effort?"

*As Quaker Prison Chaplains we saw a difference in the men's mental health during Covid, and the loss of our Quaker meetings was part of that. It gets the men off their wings, gives them some peaceful silence, and an opportunity to talk to men from other wings. The men support each other and encourage those who have not been here long and are finding it tough. This helps to foster a sense of belonging to our group.*

*It has taken a few years to get back to normal activities in prisons after Covid and this has meant slowly growing our numbers again and building back trust to enable sharing experiences of faith.*

# Describe what mental well-being means for you

D: "It's an ability to function effectively without causing long-term damage to yourself or others. It's an ability to remain calm and to manage anxieties. It's also an acceptance that things are not always as I would choose but I don't have to like them. As someone with high-functioning autism, any changes or inconsistencies that I'm not anticipating, undermine my mental health. In prison this is often caused by lack of communication.

I find singing very beneficial to my mental health. As well as singing hymns, it's being part of the Christmas Choir and taking part in workshops run by the charity *Sing Inside* who bring in volunteers to teach us songs and sing with us every few months. By the end of the day I find my confidence goes up and social anxiety goes down and feelings of self-worth improve."

P: "If I'm busy I don't ruminate and my mental health remains steady. Before I came into custody, I belonged to lots of communities but I was living a lie with skeletons in the cupboard and a drink problem. I always felt something was missing in me and most of all I felt a lack of integrity. I'm much more resilient now than when I first came into custody. The first 18 months was the toughest time in my adult life. When I'm functioning well, I feel more inclined to socialise on the wing, and only very rarely will I hide in my cell and 'lick my wounds'. I have more tactics for coping with down periods nowadays, like playing my keyboard or as a last resort just going to bed and sleeping in the hope that tomorrow will be better. The event which punctuates my week and helps to reset me is the Quaker group. On the occasions when I can't go, I usually feel something has been missed in that week."

S: "Before custody I was an alcoholic and a drug user who could not function day to day. I was abused as a child both physically and mentally; my family members knew but turned a blind eye. As I got older my mental health suffered more, my relationships failed and I was sectioned on several occasions.

Mental well-being for me now is looking after yourself both physically and in the mind. Being honest and open with yourself and your community members, it's good to talk, which this prison always encourages and most residents' doors are open to all. And we have a mental health department where we can have one to one therapy."

R: "Mental wellbeing for me means managing my emotions so that I can live my life productively. I have struggled with mental health my whole life. As a child my home environment was abusive and violent. We moved so often I could not make connections with others that could give me a sense of belonging. I suffered sexual abuse from a teacher at primary school that impacted on my lack of self-worth. It has taken many years to develop awareness within myself to recognise and identify feelings, emotions, thinking patterns and behaviours which need to be acknowledged and managed with tools and strategies so that I can cope with depression, stress or trauma triggers.

I have a journal where I write down my feelings and draw pictures to express my mood or thoughts. It is very comforting getting it out on paper. I also play guitar so it helps me identify how I'm feeling; what I play and how hard I play it, lets me know what's going on inside. I meditate, deep breathe, pray, self-gratify with food but everyone has to find what works best for them. I have a 'feelings wheel' to help with the difference between emotions and find my way to the primary emotion underneath the secondary one which is often anger.

When I do experience periods of struggle, being able to ask for help or talk about how I feel makes it easier to cope as I don't feel isolated or unvalued. I am connected to those around me and I know they will support me when I feel like I don't have the mental strength to get through it on my own."

## What does being Quaker mean to you personally and in community?

S: "Being a Quaker for me is my commitment to peace, which is also my conviction that love is at the heart of existence and that all human beings are unique and equal, trying to live honestly and with integrity, living a simple life today and helping others, and looking after the planet. Advices and Queries 1,4,11 and 22 are important to me."

R: "I am a Muslim but attend the Quaker Meetings as part of my job in the Chapel. I personally have received a great deal of care and support from Quakers and use the quiet space to reflect on life and how my life is connected to God. It is comforting to remember that we will all be tested by different challenges and it is not the end goal which is important but each step we take to reach that goal. Our strength comes from hope, and failures from our loss of it. Being part of a spiritual community reminds me of that hope."

P: "Since coming to our Quaker group I have found ways to rebuild myself from the inside-out but it's not an overnight process. I constantly work at it but as time progresses, I stumble or fall fewer times and for shorter periods so I am much more positive day to day. I smile more now and see more humour in life than I did. I still feel I have a long way to go but I don't see it as a problem anymore. Life is there for the learning.

For me being a Quaker means being more authentic as a whole person. Some on the wings take the mickey out of me and others who go to chapel but I don't let it bother me. I'd rather do what I'm doing and feel more content internally. One of my favourite things about our meeting is the feeling that although I'm 'letting go' of the past and the future, I'm still in control of now, or rather that I'm no longer out of control!"

D: "Being Quaker within our meeting gives me a sense of being part of a larger Quaker body even though our meeting is open to and includes people of any faith. Within the group I feel I can speak to the truth I see, whereas in the wider prison community I am more likely to remain silent and hope that my actions speak for me.

I and others I have spoken with, see our weekly meetings as the stable point around which the rest of the week swirls like a storm. It is the island from which we travel out, looking forward to arriving back safely at our next meeting."

# Chapter 12

## Promoting Mental Health for Family and Friends of those who are Mentally Ill

### John Miles

*This final chapter by John begins with an extraordinary family story, followed by revealing accounts of the kinds of things that can happen in a family as it absorbs the impact of living with mental illness. The six Care Pathways with which the chapter ends may constitute lessons for us all. They help us most effectively to think about ways to support Friends in our meetings who are living, day after day, year after year and decade after decade, with mental illness in the family.*

I am writing this chapter drawing from my own personal experience. I hope that it will promote greater understanding of the role of close family and friends in caring for someone with a mental illness, and how they can be upheld in that role. When someone is mentally ill, they may be a patient in a psychiatric hospital, or be cared for by a community mental health team, or perhaps living in a specialised care home. Or they may be living alone, or at home with a partner or family. For family and friends, the challenge as a Quaker is to uphold that person lovingly as best one can, however difficult, withdrawn, wayward or bizarre their behaviour. Caring for someone with a mental illness can be a tough business. You need to take care of yourself, understand your limits and set boundaries. Somehow we need to accept that mental illness, like physical illness, is just another fundamental dimension of the human condition.

## My family's story

In my lifetime three generations of my immediate family have experienced a serious mental illness in one form or another. Consequently, I am what is sometimes called "an expert by experience", having lived alongside family members with mental illness almost continuously for nearly 50 years.

## *Jack, my father*

My first close encounter with mentally illness was with my father, Jack, nearly 50 years ago. On his retirement in 1978 as a senior lecturer and head of faculty at a teacher training college, he had a significant mental breakdown. This was followed by two more episodes in later years, when for a few weeks Jack would be extremely trying to live with. This affected everyone close to him, as if a massive boulder had been cast into the middle of a pool of deep water, causing huge waves to spread out from the point of impact.

## *Simon, my brother*

Then there was my brother Simon who died in 2005. In 1980, when he was twenty-four and I was thirty-five, he was sectioned (compulsorily detained) under the Mental Health Act because of his unregulated and threatening behaviour. For twenty-five years he lived with bipolar mood disorder (also known as manic depression) with elements of post-traumatic stress disorder arising from the harsh treatment that he received when he was sectioned, involving physical restraint and forced medication. When my brother was sectioned the event was completely devastating for my mother, coming less than two years after my father's breakdown.

## *William, my son*

Last in this family trio, I would like say a little about my much-loved adult son William. Like Jack and Simon, William is highly intelligent and is prone to runaway thoughts and hypomania. In 1996 the psychiatrists made the same diagnoses as Simon's, but without the post traumatic stress disorder. William is now age 50 and has lived for more years than Simon, but with many more admissions to psychiatric hospital. Indeed, there have been so many that I have lost count.

The past decade, since 2015 has been particularly tough for William and consequently for the rest of the family. Early in 2017, in a dramatic period of mania and psychosis, he committed arson and was given a four-year sentence, two years of which were spent in prison. On his release William experienced overwhelming suicidal thoughts and made two or three serious attempts on his life. Eventually he was admitted to a specialist rehabilitation unit offering intensive psychiatric and psychological care. Although those suicidal thoughts are now much diminished, they still surface occasionally. William is now fit enough to resume a life in the community, but meantime he has been living in prison or hospital for seven years, and has become institutionalised.

# Responding to Mental Illness

My father, brother and son's mental breakdowns upset the family's equilibrium big time, causing a great deal of heartache and trauma. My mother, Margaret, likened her experience of supporting Simon to an automatic washing machine: periods of intense agitation prompted by Simon's reckless hypomanic behaviour that might go on for days, followed by comparative quiet, only for the agitation to start all over again.

These days my wife and I make a point of being open about mental illness because we think people should be made aware and understand what it can entail, for the individual experiencing it and for everyone else around. That was not something my parents and grandparents could contemplate because mental illness was something to keep quiet about, for fear of prejudice and bringing shame on the family.

The shifting dynamics of mental illness means that circumstances can change quite rapidly and often dramatically. I have learnt always to expect the unexpected – you never know what will come next! Each situation is different. For example there have been times when William has been in crisis – you might say "out of his mind" – and completely psychotic. At other times he has been clinically depressed, for days and weeks locked into an unspeakable sense of hopelessness that renders him unable to communicate. Very occasionally he is short-tempered and angry with his lot, impatient and shouting loudly in frustration, wanting to lash out. This is someone who, when he is well and on form, is charming, intelligent company, full of fun. In recent years William has become prone to panic attacks. Some situations make him so self-conscious and anxious that the only way he can regain his equilibrium is to take to his bed and sleep.

On one occasion William was at a residential conference, where early in the morning he was observed dancing on the roof of a car. The college authorities contacted me to go urgently and rescue him, which I did, but it wasn't easy. Having spent the night roaming outdoors on campus and in the nearby woods in a hypomanic state, William was emotionally disturbed, frightened and anxious. He had seen 'spirits' and an angel, and when I arrived he was outside, crouching low in self-protection. Eventually I persuaded him that my car was safe. Fortunately, in response to my pleading a bed was found for him at the psychiatric hospital that very same day and I was able to deliver him there.

A hospital admission like that would not happen these days. We would be told to go to A & E and wait patiently for triage and assessment by the mental health crisis team – incredibly difficult when the one you are with is mentally unstable, and likely to cause major disturbance to others. You have to do your best to stay calm when there is chaos all around.

On another occasion William went missing for two days from the psychiatric hospital where he was compulsorily detained as an in-patient. This was not the first time, nor the last. His illness makes him vulnerable, and on this occasion some drug addicts relieved him of his money. Oftentimes the police have been involved in locating him. In the early days, when he was living at home, we would always make a point of writing to the Police to thank them for taking care of him.

Each time William went missing, my wife and I would experience intense worry. Where was he? What on earth might happen to him? It was always a huge relief when he was found. But then there was all the hassle of getting him home, and sorting out replacements: a lost mobile phone, broken glasses, new keys, new credit cards.

Some months before he committed arson, when William was finding his life impossibly difficult, he decided on Edinburgh for a new start. With his essential and treasured possessions packed into a rucksack and two kit bags, he abandoned the key to his flat and headed for the railway station. But at Newcastle, the train divided and William had to move carriages. He forgot completely about his luggage, and arrived in Edinburgh with nothing. Later that night at about 3am, there was a call from the police to tell us he had been reported at a McDonalds near Waverley station. With support from kind-hearted Edinburgh Quakers we managed to help him return home, but just two days later he left again, this time to Liverpool. There William was taken to a police cell until a bed could be found for him at a psychiatric hospital. For two or three weeks my wife made efforts to recover his precious lost luggage from the train companies, but it was all to no avail.

## Care pathways for the carers

### Care Pathway 1: Learning and self-empowerment

Dealing with these kinds of situations can be extremely time-consuming, anxiety-provoking and distressing, not just for the sufferer but also for family and friends. Supporting someone with a mental illness can be full-on, a constant worry, at times extremely challenging. The caring skills required are quite different to that for someone with a physical disability. This was brought home to me vividly when I attended a course for carers at our local hospice. It was all about caring for people with mobility problems or who were infirm and frail, with the emphasis on physical help. With a mental illness it is the psychological and mental challenges that family and friends need to be prepared for. Carers in these circumstances need tenacity and emotionally resilience.

If this is you, there are different roles that come your way. For example, the need may be as basic as providing companionship. But for someone who is hypomanic and restless for twenty-two hours out of twenty-four, and demanding attention at all hours, it is extremely exhausting. In contrast there may be times when your loved one is feeling suicidal and isolated, full of self-loathing. I have found training in suicide prevention very helpful in knowing how to respond to the calls of desperation. But when those calls come in the middle of the night, and are repeated night after night, I am faced with a dilemma. Can I sustain that role? How much can I take? Maybe I have to impose a curfew and disconnect the phone? It's tough love and carries a risk, but for my own mental wellbeing I have to set boundaries.

Another common role is acting as an advocate for the person with the illness, dealing with their everyday affairs. For example, if your loved one is an in-patient on a psychiatric ward it can be remarkably difficult for them to have to deal with practical matters such as benefits claims, banking and paying bills, finding lost property or obtaining services. Many organisations refuse to deal with you unless they have authorisation from the person directly concerned. This needs enormous patience.

It's vital to learn how to interface with the mental health system and understand the role of key players such as the GP, the psychiatrist, the community Mental Health nurse, the patient advocate, etc. and what to do in a mental health emergency. Conversely, in a mental health emergency when the patient's records are not accessible to the team, as happens, the background information *you* have might be vital those who are responding.

It's a real blessing if you can identify a single point of contact, such as a mental health nurse who is willing to be a channel of communication. That becomes even more important if your relative is sectioned under the Mental Health Act and you find you have a statutory role as the 'nearest relative'. Fortunately, Citizens Advice and mental health charities like MIND, SANE, and Bipolar UK are on hand to give advice.

## Care Pathway 2: Prioritise your own wellbeing

It's good to be reminded that one's own mental wellbeing needs attention and maintenance. Looking after yourself is essential if you are going to do your job effectively and – indeed – you deserve it! When caring for my mentally ill father and then my brother, my mother found ways of living positively to counter being overwhelmed by her worries. In the face of seemingly unending and exhausting demands on her kindness and compassion, Margaret turned to her friends, and various creative activities that she enjoyed: cooking, spinning, listening to music, and voluntary work. Delighting in nature and the changing seasons, she recorded in her diary both the darkness and the light in her life, seeking balance. Significantly, Margaret went regularly to Quaker meeting where she might find an hour of peace and quiet for necessary rest and recovery.

My path to wellbeing was very different. After my brother's first breakdown I immersed myself in a very demanding occupation that needed my full attention, and I included regular physical exercise, walking and cycling, as part of my day. At work I could put aside my worries about parents, brother and son. Other carers practice mindfulness or Buddhist meditation, swimming, jogging or playing tennis. There are no set rules. It's just a question of finding out whatever works for you.

## Care Pathway 3: Quaker Meeting

Being accepted as part of the local Quaker meeting has been a mainstay of my own wellbeing. I have been a member of the Society of Friends from the early days of my brother's mental illness and my journey with Quakers parallels my experience of being a 'fellow traveller' first for my brother and then for my son. Attending Meeting for Worship regularly has enabled me to cope. For a quiet hour I can put events into perspective and pray for divine guidance. I often meditate on the query "What does Love require of me?".

The support of individual members of meeting has been invaluable. They ask "How is your son" and I always appreciate the inquiry. Occasionally the situation is too complex and distressing to explain in any detail. This is where the friend might reach out with a follow-up question: "How are *you* doing?" or possibly "How are you in your spirits?"

People react to stories of mental illness in different ways: with sympathy, fear, overbearing concern, benign interest and total avoidance. Some find it hard to get their head round the experiences and consequences. The capacity of a Quaker meeting to accept people who are disturbed by mental ill-health may be tested to the limit. How can we expand a meeting's caring capacity to include the mentally unwell and their family members? Perhaps it would be helpful if we can have more open conversations about mental illness and how it affects each one of us? Maybe it would help if one or two Friends in meeting can take a mental health first aid course.

## Care Pathway 4: A Listening Ear

The friend who asks "How are you doing?" is opening up an important care pathway, offering a listening ear. There is an art to listening. Spending time in the company of someone who is good at listening can be invaluable, a real tonic. Maybe there will be some dark humour about your loved one's outrageous behaviour, or a bizarre event, that relieves the tension.

Many behaviours of the mentally unwell are extreme and hard to explain, like hearing voices, self-harming and even wanting to dance on the roof of a car! The person listening to you may be curious, and have a great desire to try and make things better for you; but in my experience that kind of conversation can become intrusive and is best cut short and avoided. Some things cannot be fixed. They just have to be endured.

When living alongside the mentally ill there can be complex emotions to work through, huge anxieties and feelings of guilt. I found it essential to seek professional help from a psychotherapist in dealing with the emotional fall-out. Talking things through with a therapist helped me to put things into perspective and set some boundaries. But a therapist costs money and not everyone can afford it.

It may be that a carer's support group is available, like Al-Anon Family Groups. The organisation Bipolar UK runs family and friends support group meetings on-line once a month. These can sometimes be helpful sources of advice and offer a listening ear.

Quaker Voices on Mental Health, a Quaker Recognised Body, creates opportunities for supportive listening in our on-line small groups and on member's days. Our aim is to create a safe, on-line meeting space where people can share their vulnerabilities with other fellow-travellers and feel a sense of community. We call it "meeting on kinder ground". It requires everyone to be present for each other, willing to engage in creative listening in a non-judgemental way.

## Care Pathway 5: Prayer and Upholding

I am a great believer in the power of prayer. I pray for strength and courage in myself and the grace to forgive when I have been on the receiving end of some taxing and unreasonable behaviour. Prayer can be a great solace and a source of hope in an otherwise seemingly hopeless situation. Praying for someone or holding them in the Light and letting them know can be like holding their hand at a distance; providing a valuable sense of solidarity, companionship and community.

Some Quaker meetings arrange a 'Meeting for Healing' to focus attention on those members of the meeting who are in need of prayerful support. My own meeting has what we call an "Upholding Group". A small group of Friends connect regularly to hold in the Light members and attenders of our Meeting and their families. They do this confidentially when people are going through challenging life circumstances.

## Care Pathway 6: Pastoral Care

Pastoral Friends can help by facilitating all the other care pathways. For them a key question is "How can we be present for a family member or carer in a Quakerly and compassionate way?". Pastoral Friends need to find a balance between being supportive, but not taking on too much; being present and caring but without becoming carers. Essentially, they are the supporters of the fellow-travellers.

Pastoral Friends have to set boundaries just as family members do, especially those who are themselves mental health professionals. They can be supportive, but not prescriptive. What they say may be extremely welcome and highly relevant, but must be supplementary to the frontline professionals, who are directly responsible. And a note of caution for Pastoral Friends: families and individuals can become "invisible" to meeting through non-attendance because of everything that is going on, and then there's a risk of those individuals becoming isolated.

The Quaker community can give effective support without taking on too much. We should not underplay the value of simple practical things that might enhance someone's wellbeing, like cooking a meal, offering a lift, or occasionally offering to go in support to a mental health tribunal or other key meeting. In the words of William Penn:

*"Love is the hardest lesson in Christianity; but, for that reason, it should be most our care to learn it."*

*Quaker Faith and Practice 22.01, William Penn 1693*

# Epilogue

Is there something at the heart of this book - a golden thread that runs through all the chapters? This was the question that we asked ourselves as the chapters began to materialise.

Some years ago a young Quaker wrote: "I have come to the realisation that kindness is not a trait but a choice. The times I've felt most connected with Quakerism are when I experience kindness either from others or from myself". And Isaac Penington's words in 1667 ring down the centuries to us today:

*"Our life is love, and peace, and tenderness; and bearing one with another, and forgiving one another, and not laying accusations one against another; but praying one for another, and helping one another up with a tender hand."*

*Quaker Faith and Practice 10.01, Isaac Penington 1667*

It is a golden thread of *kindness* that runs through all these chapters, illustrating so many ways in which we can go to work for mental health. But is kindness enough? The mental health services in the NHS in Britain today are seriously under-resourced, with long delays in access to treatments, and a chronic shortage of beds for residential care. How can we honour and uphold the mentally unwell, not ignoring or overlooking them but giving them a voice?

This question is as urgent today as it was in 1792, when Friends insisted that patients should be treated with gentleness and respect. Quaker Voices on Mental Health aims to provide a national network through which Friends and Attenders can safely explore issues relating to mental illness, mental health and wellbeing in the twenty-first century. We want to see mental health services reformed in ways that are true to Quaker testimonies, and grounded in experience and action. We believe this is central to our corporate Quaker witness.